The Tragedy of Karbalā'

As narrated by Imām 'Alī ibn al-Ḥusayn as-Sajjād عليهما السلام

From the chain of narrators of Shaykh Ṣadūq
in his book *Al-Amālī*

First Published in Digital Format by The Purified Truth (Al-Ḥaqq al-Mubīn)

Translated by 'Abdul-Zahrā' 'Abdul-Ḥussain

The Tragedy of Karbalā'
As Narrated by Imam 'Alī ibn al-Ḥusayn as-Sajjād ﷺ
Translated by 'Abdul-Zahrā' 'Abdul-Ḥussain
Edited by Arifa Hudda
Typesetting and Cover Design by Saleem Bhimji

ISBN: 978-1-927930-42-7

First Printed Edition Published by:
Islamic Publishing House • www.iph.ca

Original Digital Publishing by:
The Purified Truth (*Al-Ḥaqq al-Mubīn*)

Instagram: @thepurifiedtruth
Twitter: @Purifiedtruth
Facebook: The Purified Truth - الحق المبين
YouTube: The Purified Truth

First Printed Edition by Islamic Publishing House
Under Written Permission Granted by The Purified Truth

Table of Contents

Publisher's Foreword..v

The Tragedy of Karbalā' - English Translation.............................13

The Tragedy of Karbalā' - Arabic Text...39

Our Other Publications..63

In the Name of Allah, the All-Compassionate, the All-Merciful

Publisher's Foreword[1]

قَالَ الْإِمَامُ الصَّادِقُ عليه السلام: نَفَسُ الْمَهْمُومِ لَنَا الْمُغْتَمِّ لِظُلْمِنَا تَسْبِيحٌ، وَهَمُّهُ لِأَمْرِنَا عِبَادَةٌ، وَكِتْمَانُهُ لِسِرِّنَا جِهَادٌ فِي سَبِيلِ اللّٰهِ

Imam al-Ṣādiq (ʿa) has said: "*The concerned sigh (nafas al-mahmūm) of a person who is saddened on our account and is grieved for the oppression done unto us is considered as the glorification (tasbīḥ) [of Allah]; and the grief [which a person exhibits] for our cause is*

[1] Portions of this Foreword were originally written by the Publisher for the introduction to *The Maqtal*, authored by the late Shaykh ʿAbd al-Zahrāʾ al-Kaʿbī and translated by Shaykh Usama al-Atar.

considered as the worship ('ibādat) [of Allah]; and the concealment of our secrets is struggle (jihād) in the way of Allah."[2]

That which transpired on the 10 th of Muḥarram, 61 AH was directly witnessed by the remaining members of the family of Imam al-Ḥusayn ﷺ; the opponents in the camp of Ibn Ziyād (may Allah remove His mercy from him), and the 'impartial' observers who were busy writing down what was transpiring on that tragic day. No doubt, the heartbreaking scenes were ever etched into the memory of all of those who were present there.

The moment-by-moment recount of the heroism, bravery, and valour of a small group of supporters of the truth on the side of Abā 'Abdillāh al-Ḥusayn ﷺ is a practice which started shortly after the massacre.

Prominent personalities such as Lady Zaynab binte 'Alī ﷺ, and the Imam of the time, 'Alī ibn al-Ḥusayn al-Sajjād ﷺ ensured that they availed every opportunity to remind the people about the painful narrative of Karbalā' - not only to evoke emotion in the listener, but also to ignite a spark as a vehicle for change - both personal and societal.

---

[2] Rāzī, Abū Ja'far Muḥammad ibn Ya'qūb ibn Isḥāq al-Kulaynī al-, *Al-Kāfī*, vol. 2, chap. 98, *The Book of Belief and Disbelief*, trad. 121.

They kept alive the remembrance of the painful account of what they saw, heard, and felt on the 10 th of Muḥarram, and ensured that the believers preserved it and carried it onto future generations.

The Ahlul Bayt ﷺ also encouraged their devotees to compose eulogies and poetry to stir the sentiments of those who were taking part in the gatherings *(majālis)* to remember the tragedy of Karbalā' in order to keep the memory of the oppression of the heartbreaking story of Karbalā' alive, and to remind the people about the cruelty which the Household of Prophet Muḥammad ﷺ faced by those who 'claimed' to be Muslims.

In 'Arabic, the chronicling of the narrative of the martyrdom of Imam al-Ḥusayn ibn 'Alī ﷺ is known as a *maqtal* (pl. *maqātil).* Although this is a generic term used to refer to the documenting of the specifics regarding the martyrdom of any personality, and as such countless books have been written over the centuries detailing the *maqātil* of prominent companions of Prophet Muḥammad ﷺ and other influential historical figures, however within the Shī'ī literature, this term is most associated with the writings which focus on the tragic saga of Karbalā' and the martyrdom of Abā 'Abdillāh al-Ḥusayn and his companions and family.

To date, scholars have enumerated at least 60 books within the *maqātil* genre - half of which were written about the tragedy of 'Āshūrā'. Unfortunately, due to numerous factors, many of these books are no longer in existence, and all we know about them is the author and the title of the work.

The earliest book detailing the martyrdom of Imam al-Ḥusayn ibn 'Alī is the *Maqtal of Abū Mikhnaf* which was written approximately 70 years after the tragedy of 'Āshūrā' by Abū Mikhnaf Lūṭ ibn Yaḥyā al-Azdī al-Ghāmedī (d. 157 AH).

Abū Mikhnaf was a famous historian and narrator of *aḥādīth* from the city of Kūfah, and is reported to have written 30 books including works on the Battle of Ṣiffīn, the *maqtal* of 'Uthmān b. 'Affān, the *maqtal* of Muḥammad ibn Abī Bakr, the *maqtal* of the Commander of the Faithful 'Alī ibn Abī Ṭālib , and others.

Scholars have opined that his work is one of the most authentic *maqtal* because Abū Mikhnaf lived in Kūfah during the era immediately following the tragedy of the day of 'Āshūrā', and thus was able to narrate reports either directly, or through one link in the narrator, -about what transpired on the 10 th of Muḥarram.

Although the actual text which Abū Mikhnaf compiled is no longer extant, scholars have tried their best to piece together what he may have written by relying on traditions which others quoted from books that contained narrations which he may have relied upon. As such, it should be noted that the current work known as the *Maqtal of Abū Mikhnaf* which has been translated into many languages, including English, should **not** be taken as being the original work. Those wishing to review this compilation can refer to its English translation available in print and digital format.[3]

Other books in the *maqātil* genre, which are readily available in English, include the *maqtal* of 'Alī ibn Mūsā ibn Ja'far (d. 664 AH) - Sayyid Ibn Ṭāwūs. His book, *Al-Luhūf* also known as *Al-Malhūf 'alā Qatalī al-Tufūf* is a work which many scholars refer to in their research about what transpired on the day of 'Āshūrā'.

[3] English translation is available at www.al-islam.org/event-taff-earliesthistorical-account-tragedy-karbala-abu-mikhnaf (Last accessed on August 28, 2022).

This book, *Al-Luhūf*, is divided into four parts, and starts with a preface about the greatness of the events of 'Āshūrā', the grand status of Imam al-Ḥusayn, and the value of mourning for Imam al-Ḥusayn. The first chapter reviews the events before 'Āshūrā' starting from the birth of Imam al-Ḥusayn until the day of 'Āshūrā'; the second chapter covers the events of the actual day of 'Āshūrā' until the martyrdom of Imam al-Ḥusayn; and the third chapter speaks about the events which transpired after the martyrdom of the Imam - the sending of the heads of the martyrs to Kūfah, the captivity of the Ahlul Bayt until their return to Medina. This book is available in print and online in English.[4]

Another famous *maqtal* is that of Sayyid 'Abd al-Razzāq Muḥammad al-Mūsawī al-Muqarram (d. 1971 CE). This is a lengthy book of over 400 pages which the late author wrote in 7 chapters, and organized it in the following fashion: the first section is an introduction about the uprising of Imam al-Ḥusayn; the second section reviews the narrative of Karbalā'; the third chapter speaks about Imam al-Ḥusayn and his family leaving Medina en route to Iraq; the fourth part covers

[4] English translation is available at: www.al-islam.org/lohoof-sighs-sorrowsayyid-ibn-tawus (Last accessed on August 28, 2022).

the journey from Mecca to Iraq; the fifth section details the day of ʿĀshūrāʾ; the sixth chapter highlights the martyrdom of the members of the family of Imam al-Ḥusayn 🕮 and his ultimate sacrifice; and the last part relates the events which transpired after that tragic day of ʿĀshūrāʾ. The English translation of this work is available in print and online.[5]

Lastly, we refer to the work of the late Shaykh ʿAbbās al-Qummī (d. 1940 CE), known as *Nafas al-Mahmūm fī Muṣībat Sayyidinā al-Ḥusayn al-Maẓlūm* - or *Nafas al-Mahmūm* in short.

This current publication, *The Tragedy of Karbalāʾ*, is a direct translation of the narrative of the Day of ʿĀshūrāʾ as narrated by the 4th Imam, ʿAlī ibn al-Ḥusayn Zayn al-ʿĀbidīn 🕮. This translation was carried out by ʿAbdul-Zahrāʾ ʿAbdul-Ḥussain, and was originally digitally published by *The Purified Truth (Al-Ḥaqq al-Mubīn)*. We thank him for his services in translating this valuable *ḥadīth*.

The Islamic Publishing House was then granted written permission from the Administrators of *The Purified Truth* to republish this work in print form. We are extremely grateful to *The Purified Truth* for the rights to publish this work under the

---

[5] English translation is available at: www.al-islam.org/maqtal-husayn-sayyidabd-al-razzaq-al-muqarram (Last accessed August 28, 2022).

Islamic Publishing House, and pray for their continued success in the fields of translation and propagation of the teachings of the Ahlul Bayt ﷺ. We encourage the readers of this book to follow *The Purified Truth* on social media, and support their translation projects on major books of Shīʿī literature. Their contact details can be found on the copyright page of this book.

In addition, we would like to extend our appreciation to Sr. Arifa Hudda for her editing of the English translation.

Lastly, we would like to appreciate the lovers of Abā ʿAbdillāh al-Ḥusayn ﷺ - especially those who sponsored the publication of this work.

We conclude by thanking Allāh ﷻ for allowing us to learn from the legacy of Karbalāʾ and to strive for justice in our lives. May Allah ﷻ - our Creator - join us with Imam al-Ḥusayn ﷺ and his noble family and companions, in the gardens of eternal bliss.

Saleem Bhimji

Director *of the* Islamic Publishing House

August 28th, 2022 CE

Muḥarram al-Ḥarām 30th, 1444 AH

20th Day after the Commemoration of the Tragedy of ʿĀshūrāʾ

Kitchener, Ontario, Canada

The Tragedy of Karbalā' - English Translation

In the Name of Allah, the All-Compassionate, the All- Merciful

Saturday, the 9th of Muḥarram in 386 AH is the day that coincided with the (eve of the) martyrdom of Imam al-Ḥusayn ibn ʿAlī ibn Abī Ṭālib.

The grand and virtuous scholar, Shaykh Abū Jaʿfar, Muḥammad ibn ʿAlī ibn al-Ḥusayn ibn Mūsā ibn Babāwayh al-Qummī, may Allah be pleased with him, narrated from Muḥammad ibn ʿUmar al-Baghdādī al-Ḥafīḍ, may Allah bless him, who narrated from Abū al-Saʿīd al-Ḥasan ibn ʿUthmān ibn Ziyād al-Tustarī, who narrated from the Islamic Judge of Balkh,

Ibrāhīm ibn 'Ubaydillāh ibn Mūsā ibn Yūnus ibn Abī Isḥāq al-Sabī'ī, who narrated from his aunt, Muraysa binte Mūsā ibn Yūnus ibn Abī Isḥāq, who narrated from her aunt, Ṣafiyyah binte Yūnus ibn Abī Isḥāq al-Hamdāniyyah, who narrated from her aunt, Bahjah binte al-Ḥārith ibn 'Abdullāh al-Taghlībī, who narrated from her maternal uncle, 'Abdullāh ibn Manṣūr, who was a caretaker of some of the children of Zayd ibn 'Alī, who asked Ja'far ibn Muḥammad ibn 'Alī ibn al-Ḥusayn: "Tell me about the story of the assassination of the son of Allah's Messenger ﷺ."

Imam al-Ṣādiq (a) said: "My father (al-Bāqir), has narrated to me who narrated from his father (Zayn al-'Ābidīn) who said: 'When Mu'āwiyah was approaching his death, he called upon his son Yazīd, and sat him in his presence. He said to him: 'Son, I have humiliated the necks of the people for you, and granted you the nations, and left the power and the pleasures associated with it for you.

However, I fear for you three people who will be fierce in their opposition to you, and they are: 'Abdullāh ibn 'Umar ibn al-Khaṭṭāb, 'Abdullāh ibn al-Zubayr, and al-Ḥusayn ibn 'Alī.

As for 'Abdullāh ibn 'Umar, he is with you, so take advantage of that and do not neglect him.

As for 'Abdullāh ibn al-Zubayr, if you are successful in capturing him, then cut him into pieces. If he gets the chance, he will attack you as the lion attacks their prey, for his deceitful and trickery ways will be like that of a wolf who fools a dog.

As for al-Ḥusayn ibn 'Alī, I have come to the realization of his fate from the Messenger of Allah, and he is from the flesh of the Messenger of Allah and his blood.

Undoubtedly, the people of Iraq will invite him to their lands, only to then betray him, and lose him.

If you are successful in winning him over, then be cognizant of his position and status to the Messenger of Allah, and do not punish him for his [mis]actions, as we are companions (of one another) and family, and between us are relations. Be cautions to not treat him badly, and do not let him see anything that is disliked in you..."

The 4th Imam continued to say: 'When Mu'āwiyah perished, his son Yazīd (may Allah curse him) succeeded him. He sent one of his spies to the city of the Prophet, (the spy) being his uncle 'Utbah ibn Abū Sufyān. So, he approached the city, and the governor of it was Marwān ibn al-Ḥakam, who was a spy of Mu'āwiyah.

Upon the arrival of 'Utbah, he removed Marwān from his post and sat in his place so he may fulfill the orders of Yazīd. Marwān fled the city, and 'Utbah was not able to capture him.

'Utbah called upon al-Ḥusayn ibn 'Alī and said to him: 'Indeed, the Commander of the Believers (referring to Yazīd) has ordered you to pledge allegiance to him.'

Al-Ḥusayn responded: "Utbah, you know that I belong to the Household of dignity, and we are the carriers of the Divine message. We are the banners of truth, which Allah has entrusted within our hearts, and upon which He makes us speak using our tongue by His Will.

I have heard my grandfather, the Messenger of Allah ﷺ say: 'Indeed! Caliphate is forbidden for the descendants of Abū Sufyān.

So how can I pledge allegiance to a household whom the Messenger of Allah ﷺ described as such?'

When 'Utbah heard this, he called upon a servant to write the following: 'In the Name of Allah, the All-Compassionate, the All-Merciful. To the Slave of God, Yazīd, the Commander of the Faithful. From 'Utbah ibn Abī Sufyān. Furthermore, al-Ḥusayn ibn 'Alī does not see you fit for caliphate, nor worthy of allegiance. So, order us in what you wish to do with him. Peace be upon you.'

When the letter reached Yazīd (may Allah curse him), he wrote an answer to 'Utbah saying: 'As soon as you receive my letter, hasten in writing a response to me outlining who remained in my obedience, and who deserted it. When you send your response, ensure that the head of al-Ḥusayn ibn 'Alī is alongside it.'

When al-Ḥusayn (a) heard about this, he was determined to leave the land of Ḥijāz and head towards the land of Iraq. As nighttime befell, the Imam went to the Masjid of the Prophet to bid farewell to his grandfather. When he got to the grave, a bright light radiated from the grave, which compelled him to return home.

On the second day, he went to the Masjid again to bid farewell to the Prophet. He began to pray lengthy prayers which made him sleepy. He fell asleep while he was in the state of prostration and saw the Prophet in his dream. The Prophet took al-Ḥusayn and embraced him, and began to kiss his forehead, then said: 'May my father be sacrificed for you! It is as if I see you covered in your own blood, killed by a group from this nation who seek my intercession. They will not see anything from the mercy of Allah!

O son, you will soon be reunited with your father, mother, and brother as they eagerly yearn for you.

O son, you will have such a high status in heaven, but you cannot attain that except through martyrdom.'

Al-Ḥusayn 🕮 then woke up crying. He went to his family and informed them about what happened in that dream and bid farewell to them.

He set out on a caravan composed of his brothers, his daughters, al-Qāsim ibn al-Ḥasan ibn 'Alī, alongside twenty-one of his companions and members of his household. Among them were: Abū Bakr ibn 'Alī, Muḥammad ibn 'Alī, 'Uthmān ibn 'Alī, al-'Abbās ibn 'Alī, 'Abdullāh ibn Muslim ibn 'Aqīl, 'Alī ibn al-Ḥusayn al-Akbar, and 'Alī ibn al-Ḥusayn al-Aṣghar.

'Abdullāh ibn 'Umar heard about al-Ḥusayn's departure, so he quickly followed him, and found him in some houses. He asked him: 'Where do you want to go, O son of the Messenger of Allah?'

Al-Ḥusayn answered: 'Iraq.'

'Abdullāh ibn 'Umar said: 'Do not rush, return back to the sanctuary of your grandfather.'

Al-Ḥusayn refused, and when 'Abdullāh ibn 'Umar saw that al-Ḥusayn was persistent in his refusal, 'Abdullāh said: 'O Abū 'Abdullāh, reveal the area wherein the Messenger of Allah began to kiss you.'

So, al-Ḥusayn revealed his neck. 'Abdullāh began to cry and kissed his neck three times, then said: 'I bid you farewell, O Abū 'Abdullāh, as you will be slain.'

Then, al-Ḥusayn began his journey until he reached al-Tha'libiyyah where a man by the name of Bishr ibn Ghālib came to him and said: 'O son of the Messenger of Allah, tell me about the meaning of this verse: '*On the day when We will call every nation with their leaders.*'[6]

Al-Ḥusayn replied: 'It is when a leader tries to guide the people, and they obey them; and it is when a leader calls upon deviating people, but they obey him. The former will be Heaven, while the latter will be in Hell.'

This is also the meaning behind the verse: '*A party will be in Paradise, and a party will be in the blazing Hellfire.*'[7]

---

[6] Quran. Sūrah al-Isrā' (17), verse 71:

﴿يَوْمَ نَدْعُوا۟ كُلَّ أُنَاسٍۭ بِإِمَـٰمِهِمْ ۖ ٧١﴾

[7] Quran. Sūrah al-Shūra (42), verse 7:

﴿فَرِيقٌ فِى ٱلْجَنَّةِ وَفَرِيقٌ فِى ٱلسَّعِيرِ ٧﴾

He then set out until he reached al-'Udhayb, where he took an afternoon nap, but woke up crying. His son asked him: 'O Father, what makes you cry?'

He answered: 'O son, it is a dream which I saw at an hour in which dreams cannot be untrue. A man presented an offer [to me]: to hasten in our quest [towards our eventual destiny in Karbalā'], as if we do so, we will hastily make our way to heaven.'

The Imam (and his caravan) set out until they reached al-Ruhayma, when a man from Kufa by the name of Abū Harem went to him and said: 'O son of Allah's Prophet, why did you leave Medina?'

The Imam responded: 'Woe be upon you, O Abū Harem! I was patient when they insulted my honour; and I was patient when they demanded my wealth. But they sought to shed my blood, so I fled. Allah has desired to see me killed, and this will cause them to be humiliated before Allah, killed by swords into pieces and afflicted by those who will humiliate them.'

'Ubaydillāh ibn Ziyād (may Allah ﷻ remove His mercy from him) heard about the whereabouts of al-Ḥusayn, and that he had stopped by al-Ruhayma. He appointed al-Ḥurr ibn Yazīd as commander, along with a thousand soldiers, to incapacitate al-Ḥusayn.

Al-Ḥurr said: 'When I left my home heading towards al-Ḥusayn, I heard a voice exclaiming three times: 'O Ḥurr! Glad tidings, you will enter heaven!''

I turned around and saw no one, but I thought to myself: 'May my mother be saddened by my loss! I am setting out to fight the son of Allah's Messenger and am receiving glad tidings of entering heaven?!'

He reached al-Ḥusayn at the time of the *Dhuhr* prayer. Al-Ḥusayn ordered his son to recite the *adhān* and *iqāmah*, then al-Ḥusayn led the prayers for the two camps of al-Ḥusayn and al-Ḥurr.

When al-Ḥusayn concluded, al-Ḥurr fell to al-Ḥusayn and said to him: 'Peace be upon you, O son of Allah's Messenger.'

Al-Ḥusayn responded to his greeting and asked: 'Who are you, O slave of Allah?'

He responded: 'I am al-Ḥurr ibn Yazīd.'

Al-Ḥusayn asked: 'O Ḥurr, are you with us or are you against us?'

Al-Ḥurr responded: 'By Allah, O son of Allah's Messenger, I was sent to fight you; but I seek refuge in Allah from being resurrected from the grave with my head, legs, and hands shackled to my neck, then thrown into the midst of the Hellfire.

O son of Allah's Messenger, where are you going? Return to the sanctuary of your grandfather, otherwise you will be killed.'

Al-Ḥusayn began to recite couplets of poetry in response: 'In the continuation of this journey, I shall proceed. Death will never be shame for those with truth and sincerity. With the soul, He consoles the righteous ones as He accompanies the good and opposes the criminals. If I die, there are no regrets; and if I live, I will not be blamed. As it is far better to die than live humiliated by disgrace.'

Al-Ḥusayn then set out towards al-Qatqatanah and found a built-up tent.

Al-Ḥusayn asked: 'To whom does this tent belong?'

It was said: 'It belongs to 'Ubaydillāh ibn al-Ḥurr al-Ḥanafī (al-Ju'fī).'

Al-Ḥusayn went to him and said: 'You are a sinner who is committing a grave mistake, and Allah will take your soul if you do not seek repentance to Allah in this instance. Support me, and my grandfather will intercede on your behalf to Allah.'

But he replied: 'O son of Messenger of Allah. By Allah! If I supported you, then I would be amongst the first to be killed in your way. But, take my horse of mine for you. By Allah, not a day went by where I have ridden it except that it took me to where I was striving to go, nor did an enemy ever get to me except that I saved myself with it. Take it for you.'

But al-Ḥusayn refused and said: 'I do not need you, nor your horse, as I do not take those who deviate from us as comrades. But leave this place, and do not be with us or against us. For if someone hears the cries of us - the Ahlul Bayt - and does not come to our aid, then Allah will throw that person by their face first into the fire of Hell.'

He (the Imam) then continued his journey until he reached Karbalāʾ. He asked: 'What land is this?'

It was said to him: 'This is Karbalāʾ, O son of the Messenger of Allah.'

He said: 'Indeed, this is truly a day of despair and calamities. This is the land where our blood will be shed, and where our women will be taken as captives.'

ʿUbaydillāh ibn Ziyād then entered with his army to al-Nakhḥīlah. He sent a general by the name of ʿUmar ibn Saʿad with 4,000 soldiers to al-Ḥusayn.

ʿAbdullāh ibn al-Ḥuṣayn al-Tamīmī came with 1,000 soldiers, followed by an army of 1,000 soldiers led by Shabath ibn Rabʿī, as well as Muḥammad ibn Ashʿath ibn Qays al-Kindī leading 1,000 soldiers. ‘Umar ibn Sa‘ad wrote to the people, ordering them to obey him.

‘Ubaydillāh ibn Ziyād received news that ‘Umar ibn Sa‘ad was flattering al-Ḥusayn, having conversations with him, and delaying in killing him. So ‘Ubaydillāh then sent Shimr ibn Dhil Jawshan with 4,000 soldiers and wrote to ‘Umar ibn Sa‘ad: ‘Once you receive my letter, do not delay in dealing with al-Ḥusayn ibn ‘Alī. Take advantage of his forbearance and cut the water supply from him just like it was cut from ‘Uthmān ibn al-‘Affān when he was assassinated.’

When this letter reached ‘Umar ibn Sa‘ad (may Allah curse him), he ordered a servant to call out: ‘We have given Ḥusayn and his companions this day only.’

The news reached al-Ḥusayn and his camp, and he stood up and addressed his camp saying: ‘O Lord, there is not any household more obedient (to You), purer and more purified than my household. There is not a group of companions which are better than mine. You see what has befallen me. O people, you are all excused from your allegiance towards me, and from now onwards, you do not have any allegiance on your necks towards me, and I will not hold you accountable. The night has fallen, so take it as a cover and depart confidentially in its darkness, as the enemies only want me, and when they catch me, then they will not go after anyone else.'

'Abdullāh ibn Muslim ibn 'Aqīl then stood up and said: 'O son of the Messenger of Allah, what will the people say to us if we let down our leader, our elder, our master, and the son of the greatest creation, and the son of the greatest Prophets, and did not strike a sword alongside him, nor threw a spear in his defense?! Nay by Allah! We will not leave your side, and may we sacrifice our souls and blood to safeguard yours! For if we do so, then we will have fulfilled what is obligatory upon us.'

Then a man by the name of Zuhayr ibn al-Qayn al-Bajalī stood up and said: 'O son of the Messenger of Allah, how I wish that I was killed then resurrected, then killed then resurrected, then killed then resurrected again in your sacrifice and those with you - a hundred times for the sole purpose of safeguarding you, the Ahlul Bayt.'

Al-Ḥusayn then said to him and the rest of the companions: 'May Allah reward you all with a great reward.'

Thereafter, al-Ḥusayn ordered a trench to be dug around his camp, and for it to be filled with wood.

He then sent his son 'Alī with thirty cavalier and twenty men to get water while they were in extreme thirst.

Al-Ḥusayn began reciting the following: 'O life, woe upon a friend like you! How many righteous men from around the globe have fallen dead sought out by the enemies. Indeed, it is not up to us, but the One who created. Verily, everyone shall meet their demise.'

He then told his companions: 'Drink water, as this will be your last drops of water. Do *wuḍhū* and bathe in it and wash your clothes as that will be your coffins.'

He then led them in the prayer at dawn time and prepared them for battle. He ordered the wood in the trench to be lit up with fire so the enemies could only approach them from one side.

A man from the army of 'Umar ibn Sa'ad by the name of Ibn Abī Juwayrīya al-Maznī approached. When he saw the fire, he clapped his hands and yelled out: 'O Ḥusayn and the companions of Ḥusayn! Prepare to enter the Hell fire, as you are hastening to enter it during this life!'

Al-Ḥusayn asked: 'Who is this man?'

Someone replied to him that it was Ibn Abī Juwayrīya al-Maznī, so al-Ḥusayn supplicated: 'O Allah, make him taste the punishment of the Hell fire in this world.'

Just then his horse threw him towards the flames, and he burned to death in that fire.

Then a man from the army of 'Umar ibn Sa'ad by the name of Tamīm ibn Ḥusīn al-Fazarī called out saying: 'O Ḥusayn and the companions of Ḥusayn! Do you not see the freshness of the Euphrates as it waves? By God! You will not taste even a drop from it until you die wishing for it!'

Then al-Ḥusayn asked who this man was, and someone answered him that it is Tamīm ibn Ḥusīn. Al-Ḥusayn then said: 'Him and his father will be in Hell. May Allah kill this man while he is thirsty.'

He became extremely thirsty and fell off from his horse, then his horse hit him with his legs so many times until he died.

Then another man from the army of 'Umar ibn Sa'ad by the name of Muḥammad ibn al-Ash'ath ibn Qays al-Kindī came out and said: 'O Ḥusayn, son of Fāṭima! What sort of superiority do you have that others do not have?'

Al-Ḥusayn recited the following verse: '*Indeed, Allah chose Ādam and Nūḥ, and the family of Ibrāhīm, and the family of 'Imrān over the worlds. Descendants, some of them from others...*'[8] He then

---

[8] Quran. Sūrah Āle 'Imrān (3), verses 33-34:

continued: ‘By Allah! Indeed, Muḥammad was from the progeny of Ibrāhīm, and the rightly guided progeny is from the progeny of Muḥammad. Who is this man?’

The answer was given to him that it is Muḥammad ibn al-Ash‘ath ibn Qays al-Kindī.

Al-Ḥusayn then raised his head towards the skies and said: ‘O Allah, humiliate Muḥammad ibn al-Ash‘ath on this day, and do not give him honour after today.’

He then left the battlefield, and Allah afflicted him (Muḥammad ibn al-Ash‘ath) with a scorpion that struck him until he died nude.

Thirst started to overtake al-Ḥusayn and his companions. A man from his Shī‘a by the name of Burayr ibn Khudayr al-Hamadānī entered upon him. The narrator, Ibrāhīm ibn ‘Abdullāh said that he was the uncle of Abī Isḥāq al-Hamadānī.

Burayr asked (al-Ḥusayn): ‘Do you grant me permission to go and address them?’

Al-Ḥusayn granted him permission, so Burayr went out and said: ‘O People! Indeed, Allah sent Muḥammad with the truth,

---

﴿إِنَّ ٱللَّهَ ٱصۡطَفَىٰٓ ءَادَمَ وَنُوحٗا وَءَالَ إِبۡرَٰهِيمَ وَءَالَ عِمۡرَٰنَ عَلَى ٱلۡعَٰلَمِينَ ٣٣ ذُرِّيَّةَۢ بَعۡضُهَا مِنۢ بَعۡضٖۗ ٣٤﴾

as a Messenger and a Warner and a Caller to Allah. Here is the Euphrates, surrounded by pigs and dogs.'

They said: 'O Burayr, you have talked too much, enough now. By Allah, Ḥusayn will remain thirsty just like those before him.'

Al-Ḥusayn asked Burayr to come and sit down, then he (al-Ḥusayn) stood up using his sword and called out: 'I ask you by Allah! Do you know who I am?'

They (the enemies) replied: 'Yes, you are the son of the Messenger of Allah and his grandson.'

He continued: 'I ask you by Allah, do you know that my grandfather is the Messenger of Allah?'

They answered: 'By Allah, yes!'

He went on: 'I ask you by Allah, do you know that my mother is Fāṭima binte Muḥammad?'

They replied: 'By Allah, yes!'

He questioned them: 'I ask you by Allah, do you know that my father is 'Alī ibn Abī Ṭālib?'

They said: 'By Allah, yes!'

He continued: 'I ask you by Allah, do you know that my grandmother is Khadījah binte Khuwaylid, who was the first woman to become a Muslim?'

They answered: 'By Allah, yes!'

He then said: 'I ask you by Allah, do you know that the Master of Martyrs, Hamza is my father's uncle?'

They replied: 'By Allah, yes!'

Then he asked them: 'I ask you by Allah, do you know that my uncle Ja'far al-Ṭayyār is in Heaven?'

They said: 'By Allah, yes!'

Al-Ḥusayn then said: 'I ask you by Allah, is this not the sword of the Messenger of Allah that I am carrying?'

They answered: 'By Allah, yes!'

He continued: 'I ask you by Allah, is this not the turban of the Messenger of Allah that I am wearing?'

They replied: 'By Allah, yes!'

He further asked them: 'I ask you by Allah, was 'Alī not the first Muslim, the most knowledgeable, the most forbearing, and the master of every believer?'

They said: 'By Allah, yes!'

He continued: 'Then for what reason do you want to shed my blood, when my father is the one who will feed the people from the Heavenly pond (in the next world), just like a thirsty camel is fed, while the banner will be carried by my grandfather on the Day of Judgement?'

They replied: 'We know all of this, but despite that we will not leave you until you are killed thirsty.'

Then al-Ḥusayn held a portion of his beard, and he was 57 years old at the time, and said: 'Allah became angry at the Jews when they claimed that 'Uzayr was the son of Allah; and Allah became angry at the Christians when they claimed that 'Isā was the son of Allah. Allah became angry at the Zoroastrians when they worshipped the fire instead of Allah; and He became angry at the people when they killed their Prophet; and Allah will become angry with these people as they want to kill the son of their Prophet.'

Then al-Ḥurr ibn Yazīd got on his horse and deserted the army of 'Umar ibn Sa'ad and joined the camp of al-Ḥusayn. He entered with his hand covering his head and said: 'O Allah, I beseech you to grant me repentance, as the hearts of Your righteous servants and the children of Your Prophet have become horrified. O son of Allah's Messenger, am I worthy of repentance?'

Al-Ḥusayn responded: 'Yes, Allah has forgiven you.'

Al-Ḥurr said: 'O son of the Messenger of Allah, do you grant me permission to fight them?'

Al-Ḥusayn granted him permission, so he went out and recited: 'I will strike my sword upon your necks, in defense of the greatest man to set forth on these lands.'

He then killed eighteen people until he himself was killed.

Al-Ḥusayn went to him while al-Ḥurr was bleeding and said to him: 'Glad tidings O Ḥurr, you are a free man just like you were named - in this life and the hereafter.'

Al-Ḥusayn recited this poem in his praise: 'Praise be upon Ḥurr, the free man from the Tribe of Riyāḥ; he is al-Ḥurr, skilled in the art of spears. Praise be upon Ḥurr, who called upon Ḥusayn, and found him amongst his midst after dawn had fallen.'

Then Zuhayr ibn al-Qayn al-Bajalī entered the battlefield to fight and addressed al-Ḥusayn saying: 'Today is the day of reunion, as we meet your grandfather, al-Murtaḍā, and al-Ḥasan.'

He killed nineteen soldiers from the enemies. When he was struck with a fatal blow, he exclaimed: 'I am Zuhayr, the son of al-Qayn, with my sword I will fight those who fight al-Ḥusayn!'

Then Ḥabīb ibn Mudhāhir al-Asadī entered the battlefield saying: 'I am Ḥabīb, the son of Mudhāhir, we are wiser than them and purer, and we are the supporters of the best of humankind!'

After his recitation, he killed thirty soldiers from the enemies until he was killed. Then 'Abdullāh ibn Abī 'Urwah al-Ghaffārī entered the battlefield. He said: 'I have come to know the truth of Banī al-Ghaffār, and I have gone to seek revenge in al-Mashrafī, and [there] I was taught the use of a spear!'

He killed twenty soldiers from the enemies until he passed away, may Allah's mercy be upon him.

Then Burayr ibn Khudayr al-Hamadānī, who was the most knowledgeable of his era, entered the battlefield saying: 'I am Burayr, and my father is Khudayr; no goodness to those who do not display goodness today.'

He killed thirty soldiers from the enemies until he was killed, may Allah be pleased with him.

Then Mālik ibn Anas went out and said: 'I have come to know the [difference between the] household [of Allah)] and the worms, and the [difference between the] children of Ilyās and the standard children, and my people are those who dismantle our opposition. O people, be like lions protecting the family of

'Alī, and the Shī'a of al-Raḥmān, and the family of Harb[9] are the Shī'a of Shaytān.'

He then killed eighteen soldiers from the enemies until he was killed, may Allah be pleased with him.

Then Ziyād ibn Mahāsir al-Kindī went out and said: 'I am Ziyād, son of Mahasīr. I am the brave warrior fighting, and the Lord of Ḥusayn I am supporting; and Ibn Sa'ad I am neglecting.'

He killed nine soldiers until he was killed, may Allah bless him.

Then Wahab ibn Wahab went out, he and his mother were Christians who became Muslims under the hands of al-Ḥusayn.

He and his mother accompanied al-Ḥusayn to Karbalā', then he rode a horse carrying a wooden stick and began to fight the enemies until he killed seven or eight soldiers. He then went to rest for a bit when 'Umar ibn Sa'ad ordered a solider to decapitate him. He was decapitated and his head was thrown to the camp of al-Ḥusayn. His mother picked up his sword and wanted to fight, but al-Ḥusayn said: 'O Umm (mother of) Wahab, sit down, as Allah has not made *jihād* (fighting on the battlefield) obligatory upon women. Verily, you and your son will be with my grandfather, the Messenger of Allah, in Heaven.'

---

[9] This is a reference to the family of Abū Sufyān.

Then Hilāl ibn Ḥajjāj went out and said: 'Throw (the spears) with knowledge over into the air, as my soul will not gain benefit from your pity!'

He then killed thirteen soldiers until he himself was killed; may Allah be pleased with him.

Then 'Abdullāh ibn Muslim ibn 'Aqīl went out and said: 'I vowed not to die but as a free man; and I found death to be undesirable when I am called upon it as I flee. As the coward is the one who runs away and flees.'

He killed three of them until he was killed, may Allah be pleased with him.

Then 'Alī ibn Ḥusayn al-Akbar went out. As he got out to fight, al-Ḥusayn began to shed tears and said: 'O Allah, be the witness over them as he is the son of Allah's Messenger, and the man who resembles him the most in terms of manners and appearance has gone out to fight them.'

As he left to fight, he said: 'I am 'Alī ibn al-Ḥusayn ibn 'Alī, we belong to the House of Allah and the Prophet; do you not see how I will defend my father?'

He killed ten of the soldiers, then went back to his father and said: 'O father, I am so thirsty!'

Al-Ḥusayn responded: 'Be patient, O son, your grandfather will feed you water.'

He returned to fight and killed forty-four people until he himself got killed, may Allah be pleased with him.

Then al-Qāsim ibn al-Ḥasan ibn 'Alī ibn Abī Ṭālib went out and said: 'O soul, do not despair over yourself, as shortly you shall be granted Heaven by His Majesty.'

He killed three soldiers until he himself was killed; may Allah be pleased with him.

Al-Ḥusayn then stood all alone looking around, but he saw no one by his side. He then looked towards the skies and said: 'O Allah, You see what is happening to the son of Your Prophet.'

Then some of the soldiers went in between him and the river, and a soldier threw an arrow which landed on his neck. He then fell off his horse.

He held the arrow and pulled it out as blood began to gush out. He held out his palm to intercept the blood as it was coming out, and when it got full, he covered his face and beard with it, then said: 'This is how I shall meet my Lord, as I am covered in my own blood.'

He then fell and landed on his left cheek. The enemies of Allah, Sinān ibn Anas al-Ayādī and Shimr ibn Dhil Jawshan (may Allah curse them both) came with a group of people from the Levant and stood by the head of al-Ḥusayn.

They began to say to each other: 'What are you waiting for, put him out his misery!'

Sinān ibn Anas al-Ayādī came down and held the beard of al-Ḥusayn and began to hit his mouth with his sword and said to him: 'By Allah! I will cut off your head despite knowing that you are the son of Allah's Messenger and have the best mother and father.'

The horse of al-Ḥusayn came and covered its head and back with the blood of al-Ḥusayn. The horse began to neigh and nicker as it ran around, and the women of the Prophet heard his cries and came out (of the tents) to find the horse without its master, and this is when they discovered that al-Ḥusayn had been killed.

Then Umm Kulthūm binte al-Ḥusayn came out and placed her hand on the head of al-Ḥusayn and began to lament saying: '*Wah Muḥammadah* (O Muḥammad)! This is Ḥusayn all alone, with his robe and turban torn off!'

Sinān then entered the court of 'Ubaydillāh ibn Ziyād and presented him with the decapitated head of al-Ḥusayn ibn 'Alī while reciting: 'Fill gold and silver around my knees as I have killed the notorious king, whose greatest lineage cannot be matched as he had the best mother and father.'

'Ubaydillāh ibn Ziyād said: 'Woe be upon you! If you know that he had the best mother and father, then why did you kill him?!'

He ('Ubaydillāh) gave an order for his (Sinān's) execution, and Allah hastened to send him to Hell, his eternal abode.

Ibn Ziyād then went to Umm Kulthūm[10] the daughter (or sister) of al-Ḥusayn and said: 'Praise be to Allah who killed your men, how do you find what happened to you?'

She replied: 'O Ibn Ziyād, if you are joyous over the killing of al-Ḥusayn, then know that you have reunited him with his grandfather, the Messenger of Allāh, as he used to kiss al-Ḥusayn and embrace him immensely. O Ibn Ziyād, go prepare an answer for his grandfather as you will be his enemy on the Day of Judgement.'"

May the peace and blessings be upon Muḥammad and his progeny.

---

[10] The Arabic text makes note that this Umm Kulthūm could be the daughter or sister of Imam al-Ḥusayn ▧.

The Tragedy of Karbalāʾ - Arabic Text

حَدَّثَنَا الشَّيْخُ الْفَقِيهُ أَبُو جَعْفَرٍ مُحَمَّدُ بْنُ عَلِيٍّ بْنِ الْحُسَيْنِ بْنِ مُوسَى بْنِ بَابَوَيْهِ الْقُمِّيُّ رَحِمَهُ اللَّهُ قَالَ حَدَّثَنَا مُحَمَّدُ بْنُ عُمَرَ الْبَغْدَادِيُّ الْحَافِظُ رَحِمَهُ اللَّهُ قَالَ حَدَّثَنَا أَبُو سَعِيدٍ الْحَسَنُ بْنُ عُثْمَانَ بْنِ زِيَادٍ التُّسْتَرِيُّ مِنْ كِتَابِهِ قَالَ حَدَّثَنَا إِبْرَاهِيمُ بْنُ عُبَيْدِ اللَّهِ بْنِ مُوسَى بْنِ يُونُسَ بْنِ أَبِي إِسْحَاقَ السَّبِيعِيُّ قَاضِي بَلْخٍ قَالَ حَدَّثَتْنِي مُرَيْسَةُ بِنْتُ مُوسَى بْنِ يُونُسَ بْنِ أَبِي إِسْحَاقَ وَكَانَتْ عَمَّتِي قَالَتْ حَدَّثَتْنِي صَفِيَّةُ

بِنْتُ يُونُسَ بْنِ أَبِي إِسْحَاقَ الْهَمْدَانِيَّةُ وَكَانَتْ عَمَّتِي قَالَتْ حَدَّثَتْنِي بَهْجَةُ بِنْتُ الْحَارِثِ بْنِ عَبْدِ اللّٰهِ التَّغْلِبِيُّ عَنْ خَالِهَا عَبْدِ اللّٰهِ بْنِ مَنْصُورٍ وَكَانَ رَضِيعًا لِبَعْضِ وُلْدِ زَيْدِ بْنِ عَلِيٍّ عليهما السلام قَالَ: سَأَلْتُ جَعْفَرَ بْنَ مُحَمَّدِ بْنِ عَلِيِّ بْنِ الْحُسَيْنِ عليهم السلام فَقُلْتُ حَدِّثْنِي عَنْ مَقْتَلِ ابْنِ رَسُولِ اللّٰهِ صلى الله عليه وآله وسلم.

فَقَالَ حَدَّثَنِي أَبِي عَنْ أَبِيهِ قَالَ:

لَمَّا حَضَرَتْ مُعَاوِيَةَ الْوَفَاةُ دَعَا ابْنَهُ يَزِيدَ لَعَنَهُ اللّٰهُ فَأَجْلَسَهُ بَيْنَ يَدَيْهِ فَقَالَ لَهُ يَا بُنَيَّ إِنِّي قَدْ ذَلَّلْتُ لَكَ الرِّقَابَ الصِّعَابَ وَوَطَّدْتُ لَكَ الْبِلَادَ وَجَعَلْتُ الْمُلْكَ وَمَا فِيهِ لَكَ طُعْمَةً.

وَإِنِّي أَخْشَى عَلَيْكَ مِنْ ثَلَاثَةِ نَفَرٍ يُخَالِفُونَ عَلَيْكَ بِجَهْدِهِمْ وَهُمْ عَبْدُ اللّٰهِ بْنُ عُمَرَ بْنِ الْخَطَّابِ وَعَبْدُ اللّٰهِ بْنُ الزُّبَيْرِ وَالْحُسَيْنُ بْنُ عَلِيٍّ.

فَأَمَّا عَبْدُ اللّٰهِ بْنُ عُمَرَ فَهُوَمَعَكَ فَالْزَمْهُ وَلَا تَدعْهُ.

وَأَمَّا عَبْدُ اللّٰهِ بْنُ الزُّبَيْرِ فَقَطِّعْهُ إِنْ ظَفِرْتَ بِهِ إِرْبًا إِرْبًا فَإِنَّهُ يَجْثُو لَكَ كَمَا يَجْثُو الْأَسَدُ لِفَرِيسَتِهِ وَيُوَارِبُكَ مُوَارَبَةَ الثَّعْلَبِ لِلْكَلْبِ.

وَأَمَّا الْحُسَيْنُ عليه السلام فَقَدْ عَرَفْتَ حَظَّهُ مِنْ رَسُولِ اللّٰهِ صلى الله عليه وآله وسلم وَهُوَ مِنْ لَحْمِ رَسُولِ اللّٰهِ وَدَمِهِ.

وَقَدْ عَلِمْتُ لَا مَحَالَةَ أَنَّ أَهْلَ الْعِرَاقِ سَيُخْرِجُونَهُ إِلَيْهِمْ ثُمَّ يَخْذُلُونَهُ وَيُضَيِّعُونَهُ.

فَإِنْ ظَفِرْتَ بِهِ فَاعْرِفْ حَقَّهُ وَمَنْزِلَتَهُ مِنْ رَسُولِ اللّٰهِ ﷺ وَلَا تُؤَاخِذْهُ بِفِعْلِهِ وَمَعَ ذٰلِكَ فَإِنَّ لَنَا بِهِ خِلْطَةً وَرَحِما وَإِيَّاكَ أَنْ تَنَالَهُ بِسُوءٍ وَيَرَى مِنْكَ مَكْرُوهًا.

قَالَ فَلَمَّا هَلَكَ مُعَاوِيَةُ وَتَوَلَّى الْأَمْرَ بَعْدَهُ يَزِيدُ بَعَثَ عَامِلَهُ عَلَى مَدِينَةِ رَسُولِ اللّٰهِ وَهُوَ عَمُّهُ عُتْبَةُ بْنُ أَبِي سُفْيَانَ فَقَدِمَ الْمَدِينَةَ وَعَلَيْهَا مَرْوَانُ بْنُ الْحَكَمِ وَكَانَ عَامِلَ مُعَاوِيَةَ.

فَأَقَامَهُ عُتْبَةُ مِنْ مَكَانِهِ وَجَلَسَ فِيهِ لِيُنْفِذَ فِيهِ أَمْرَ يَزِيدَ فَهَرَبَ مَرْوَانُ فَلَمْ يَقْدِرْ عَلَيْهِ.

وَبَعَثَ عُتْبَةُ إِلَى الْحُسَيْنِ بْنِ عَلِيٍّ فَقَالَ إِنَّ أَمِيرَ الْمُؤْمِنِينَ أَمَرَكَ أَنْ تُبَايِعَ لَهُ.

فَقَالَ الْحُسَيْنُ عليه السلام يَا عُتْبَةُ قَدْ عَلِمْتَ أَنَّا أَهْلُ بَيْتِ الْكَرَامَةِ وَمَعْدِنُ الرِّسَالَةِ وَأَعْلَامُ الْحَقِّ الَّذِينَ أَوْدَعَهُ اللّٰهِ عز وجل قُلُوبَنَا وَأَنْطَقَ بِهِ أَلْسِنَتَنَا فَنَطَقَتْ بِإِذْنِ اللّٰهِ عز وجل.

وَلَقَدْ سَمِعْتُ جَدِّي رَسُولَ اللّٰهِ ﷺ يَقُولُ إِنَّ الْخِلَافَةَ مُحَرَّمَةٌ عَلَى وُلْدِ أَبِي سُفْيَانَ.

وَكَيْفَ أُبَايِعُ أَهْلَ بَيْتٍ قَدْ قَالَ فِيهِمْ رَسُولُ اللّٰهِ ﷺ هٰذَا.

فَلَمَّا سَمِعَ عُتْبَةُ ذٰلِكَ دَعَا الْكَاتِبَ وَكَتَبَ بِسْمِ اللّٰهِ الرَّحْمٰنِ الرَّحِيمِ إِلَى عَبْدِ اللّٰهِ يَزِيدَ أَمِيرِ الْمُؤْمِنِينَ مِنْ عُتْبَةَ بْنِ أَبِي سُفْيَانَ أَمَّا بَعْدُ فَإِنَّ الْحُسَيْنَ بْنَ عَلِيٍّ لَيْسَ يَرَى لَكَ خِلَافَةً وَلَا بَيْعَةً فَرَأْيُكَ فِي أَمْرِهِ وَالسَّلَامُ.

فَلَمَّا وَرَدَ الْكِتَابُ عَلَى يَزِيدَ لَعَنَهُ اللّٰهِ كَتَبَ الْجَوَابَ إِلَى عُتْبَةَ: أَمَّا بَعْدُ فَإِذَا أَتَاكَ كِتَابِي هٰذَا فَعَجِّلْ عَلَيَّ بِجَوَابِهِ وَبَيِّنْ لِي فِي كِتَابِكَ كُلَّ مَنْ فِي طَاعَتِي أَوْ خَرَجَ عَنْهَا وَلْيَكُنْ مَعَ الْجَوَابِ رَأْسُ الْحُسَيْنِ بْنِ عَلِيٍّ.

فَبَلَغَ ذٰلِكَ الْحُسَيْنَ فَهَمَّ بِالْخُرُوجِ مِنْ أَرْضِ الْحِجَازِ إِلَى أَرْضِ الْعِرَاقِ فَلَمَّا أَقْبَلَ اللَّيْلُ رَاحَ إِلَى مَسْجِدِ النَّبِيِّ ﷺ لِيُوَدِّعَ الْقَبْرَ فَلَمَّا وَصَلَ إِلَى الْقَبْرِ سَطَعَ لَهُ نُورٌ مِنَ الْقَبْرِ فَعَادَ إِلَى مَوْضِعِهِ.

فَلَمَّا كَانَتِ اللَّيْلَةُ الثَّانِيَةُ رَاحَ لِيُوَدِّعَ الْقَبْرَ فَقَامَ يُصَلِّي فَأَطَالَ فَنَعَسَ وَهُوَ سَاجِدٌ فَجَاءَهُ النَّبِيُّ ﷺ وَهُوَ فِي مَنَامِهِ فَأَخَذَ الْحُسَيْنَ

ﷺ وَضَمَّهُ إِلَى صَدْرِهِ وَجَعَلَ يُقَبِّلُ عَيْنَيْهِ وَيَقُولُ بِأَبِي أَنْتَ كَأَنِّي أَرَاكَ مُرَمَّلًا بِدَمِكَ بَيْنَ عِصَابَةٍ مِنْ هٰذِهِ الْأُمَّةِ يَرْجُونَ شَفَاعَتِي مَا لَهُمْ عِنْدَ اللّٰهِ مِنْ خَلَاقٍ.

يَا بُنَيَّ إِنَّكَ قَادِمٌ عَلَى أَبِيكَ وَأُمِّكَ وَأَخِيكَ وَهُمْ مُشْتَاقُونَ إِلَيْكَ وَإِنَّ لَكَ فِي الْجَنَّةِ دَرَجَاتٍ لَا تَنَالُهَا إِلَّا بِالشَّهَادَةِ.

فَانْتَبَهَ الْحُسَيْنُ عليه السلام مِنْ نَوْمِهِ بَاكِيًا فَأَتَى أَهْلَ بَيْتِهِ فَأَخْبَرَهُمْ بِالرُّؤْيَا وَوَدَّعَهُمْ وَحَمَلَ أَخَوَاتِهِ عَلَى الْمَحَامِلِ وَابْنَتَهُ وَابْنَ أَخِيهِ الْقَاسِمَ بْنَ الْحَسَنِ بْنِ عَلِيٍّ عليهم السلام ثُمَّ سَارَ فِي أَحَدٍ وَعِشْرِينَ رَجُلًا مِنْ أَصْحَابِهِ وَأَهْلِ بَيْتِهِ مِنْهُمْ أَبُو بَكْرِ بْنُ عَلِيٍّ وَمُحَمَّدُ بْنُ عَلِيٍّ وَعُثْمَانُ بْنُ عَلِيٍّ وَالْعَبَّاسُ بْنُ عَلِيٍّ وَعَبْدُ اللّٰهِ بْنُ مُسْلِمِ بْنِ عَقِيلٍ وَعَلِيُّ بْنُ الْحُسَيْنِ الْأَكْبَرُ وَعَلِيُّ بْنُ الْحُسَيْنِ الْأَصْغَرُ عليهم السلام.

وَسَمِعَ عَبْدُ اللّٰهِ بْنُ عُمَرَ بِخُرُوجِهِ فَقَدَّمَ رَاحِلَتَهُ وَخَرَجَ خَلْفَهُ مُسْرِعًا فَأَدْرَكَهُ فِي بَعْضِ الْمَنَازِلِ فَقَالَ أَيْنَ تُرِيدُ يَا ابْنَ رَسُولِ اللّٰهِ.

قَالَ الْعِرَاقَ.

قَالَ مَهْلًا ارْجِعْ إِلَى حَرَمِ جَدِّكَ.

فَأَبَى الْحُسَيْنُ ﷺ عَلَيْهِ فَلَمَّا رَأَى ابْنُ عُمَرَ إِبَاءَهُ قَالَ يَا أَبَا عَبْدِ اللّٰهِ اكْشِفْ لِي عَنِ الْمَوْضِعِ الَّذِي كَانَ رَسُولُ اللّٰهِ ﷺ يُقَبِّلُهُ مِنْكَ.

فَكَشَفَ الْحُسَيْنُ ﷺ عَنْ سُرَّتِهِ فَقَبَّلَهَا ابْنُ عُمَرَ ثَلَاثًا وَبَكَى وَقَالَ أَسْتَوْدِعُكَ اللّٰهِ يَا أَبَا عَبْدِ اللّٰهِ فَإِنَّكَ مَقْتُولٌ فِي وَجْهِكَ هٰذَا.

فَسَارَ الْحُسَيْنُ ﷺ وَأَصْحَابُهُ فَلَمَّا نَزَلُوا ثَعْلَبِيَّةَ وَرَدَ عَلَيْهِ رَجُلٌ يُقَالُ لَهُ بِشْرُ بْنُ غَالِبٍ فَقَالَ يَا ابْنَ رَسُولِ اللّٰهِ ﷺ أَخْبِرْنِي عَنْ قَوْلِ اللّٰهِ ﷻ يَوْمَ نَدْعُوا كُلَّ أُنَاسٍ بِإِمَامِهِمْ.

قَالَ إِمَامٌ دَعَا إِلَى هُدًى فَأَجَابُوهُ إِلَيْهِ وَإِمَامٌ دَعَا إِلَى ضَلَالَةٍ فَأَجَابُوهُ إِلَيْهَا هَؤُلَاءِ فِي الْجَنَّةِ وَهَؤُلَاءِ فِي النَّارِ.

وَهُوَ قَوْلُهُ ﷻ فَرِيقٌ فِي الْجَنَّةِ وَفَرِيقٌ فِي السَّعِيرِ.

ثُمَّ سَارَ حَتَّى نَزَلَ الْعُذَيْبَ فَقَالَ فِيهَا قَائِلَةَ الظَّهِيرَةِ ثُمَّ انْتَبَهَ مِنْ نَوْمِهِ بَاكِيًا فَقَالَ لَهُ ابْنُهُ مَا يُبْكِيكَ يَا أَبَتِ.

فَقَالَ يَا بُنَيَّ إِنَّهَا سَاعَةٌ لَا تَكْذِبُ الرُّؤْيَا فِيهَا وَإِنَّهُ عَرَضَ لِي فِي مَنَامِي عَارِضٌ فَقَالَ تُسْرِعُونَ السَّيْرَ وَالْمَنَايَا تَسِيرُ بِكُمْ إِلَى الْجَنَّةِ.

ثُمَّ سَارَ حَتَّى نَزَلَ الرُّهَيْمَةَ فَوَرَدَ عَلَيْهِ رَجُلٌ مِنْ أَهْلِ الْكُوفَةِ يُكَنَّى أَبَا هَرِمٍ فَقَالَ يَا ابْنَ النَّبِيِّ مَا الَّذِي أَخْرَجَكَ مِنَ الْمَدِينَةِ.

فَقَالَ وَيْحَكَ يَا أَبَا هَرِمٍ شَتَمُوا عِرْضِي فَصَبَرْتُ وَطَلَبُوا مَالِي فَصَبَرْتُ وَطَلَبُوا دَمِي فَهَرَبْتُ وَايْمُ اللّٰهِ لَيَقْتُلُنِي ثُمَّ لَيَلْبَسَنَّهُمُ اللّٰهُ ذُلًّا شَامِلًا وَسَيْفًا قَاطِعًا وَلَيُسَلِّطَنَّ عَلَيْهِمْ مَنْ يُذِلُّهُمْ.

قَالَ وَبَلَغَ عُبَيْدَ اللّٰهِ بْنَ زِيَادٍ لَعَنَهُ اللّٰهُ الْخَبَرُ وَأَنَّ الْحُسَيْنَ عليه السلام قَدْ نَزَلَ الرُّهَيْمِيَّةَ [الرهمية [الرُّهَيْمَةَ]] فَأَرْسَلَ إِلَيْهِ الْحُرَّ بْنَ يَزِيدَ فِي أَلْفِ فَارِسٍ.

قَالَ الْحُرُّ فَلَمَّا خَرَجْتُ مِنْ مَنْزِلِي مُتَوَجِّهًا نَحْوَ الْحُسَيْنِ عليه السلام نُودِيتُ ثَلَاثًا يَا حُرُّ أَبْشِرْ بِالْجَنَّةِ.

فَالْتَفَتُّ فَلَمْ أَرَ أَحَدًا فَقُلْتُ ثَكِلَتِ الْحُرَّ أُمُّهُ يَخْرُجُ إِلَى قِتَالِ ابْنِ رَسُولِ اللّٰهِ صلى الله عليه وآله وَيُبَشَّرُ بِالْجَنَّةِ.

فَرَهِقَهُ عِنْدَ صَلَاةِ الظُّهْرِ فَأَمَرَ الْحُسَيْنُ عليه السلام ابْنَهُ فَأَذَّنَ وَأَقَامَ وَقَامَ الْحُسَيْنُ عليه السلام فَصَلَّى بِالْفَرِيقَيْنِ جَمِيعًا.

فَلَمَّا سَلَّمَ وَثَبَ الْحُرُّ بْنُ يَزِيدَ فَقَالَ السَّلَامُ عَلَيْكَ يَا ابْنَ رَسُولِ اللّٰهِ وَرَحْمَةُ اللّٰهِ وَبَرَكَاتُهُ.

فَقَالَ الْحُسَيْنُ عليه السلام وَعَلَيْكَ السَّلَامُ مَنْ أَنْتَ يَا عَبْدَ اللّٰهِ.

فَقَالَ أَنَا الْحُرُّ بْنُ يَزِيدَ.

فَقَالَ يَا حُرُّ أَ عَلَيْنَا أَمْ لَنَا.

فَقَالَ الْحُرُّ وَاللهِ يَا ابْنَ رَسُولِ اللهِ لَقَدْ بُعِثْتُ لِقِتَالِكَ وَأَعُوذُ بِاللهِ أَنْ أُحْشَرَ مِنْ قَبْرِي وَنَاصِيَتِي مَشْدُودَةٌ إِلَى رِجْلِي وَيَدَيَّ مَغْلُولَةٌ إِلَى عُنُقِي وَأُكَبَّ عَلَى حُرِّ وَجْهِي فِي النَّارِ يَا ابْنَ رَسُولِ اللهِ أَيْنَ تَذْهَبُ ارْجِعْ إِلَى حَرَمِ جَدِّكَ فَإِنَّكَ مَقْتُولٌ.

فَقَالَ الْحُسَيْنُ عليه السلام:

سَأَمْضِي فَمَا بِالْمَوْتِ عَارٌ عَلَى الْفَتَى إِذَا مَا نَوَى حَقًّا وَجَاهَدَ مُسْلِمًا
وَوَاسَى الرِّجَالَ الصَّالِحِينَ بِنَفْسِهِ وَفَارَقَ مَثْبُورًا وَخَالَفَ مُجْرِمًا
فَإِنْ مِتُّ لَمْ أَنْدَمْ وَإِنْ عِشْتُ لَمْ أُلَمْ كَفَى بِكَ ذُلًّا أَنْ تَمُوتَ وَتُرْغَمَا

ثُمَّ سَارَ الْحُسَيْنُ عليه السلام حَتَّى نَزَلَ الْقُطْقُطَانِيَّةَ فَنَظَرَ إِلَى فُسْطَاطٍ مَضْرُوبٍ.

فَقَالَ لِمَنْ هٰذَا الْفُسْطَاطُ.

فَقِيلَ لِعُبَيْدِ اللهِ بْنِ الْحُرِّ الْحَنَفِيِّ [الْجُعْفِيِّ].

فَأَرْسَلَ إِلَيْهِ الْحُسَيْنُ عليه السلام فَقَالَ أَيُّهَا الرَّجُلُ إِنَّكَ مُذْنِبٌ خَاطِئٌ إِنَّ اللهَ عَزَّ وَجَلَّ آخِذُكَ بِمَا أَنْتَ صَانِعٌ إِنْ لَمْ تَتُبْ إِلَى اللهِ تَبَارَكَ وَتَعَالَى

فِي سَاعَتِكَ هٰذِهِ فَتَنْصُرَنِي وَيَكُونَ جَدِّي شَفِيعَكَ بَيْنَ يَدَيِ اللّٰهِ تَبَارَكَ وَتَعَالَى.

فَقَالَ يَا ابْنَ رَسُولِ اللّٰهِ وَاللّٰهِ لَوْ نَصَرْتُكَ لَكُنْتُ أَوَّلَ مَقْتُولٍ بَيْنَ يَدَيْكَ وَلَكِنَّ هٰذَا فَرَسِي خُذْهُ إِلَيْكَ فَوَاللّٰهِ مَا رَكِبْتُهُ قَطُّ وَأَنَا أَرُومُ شَيْئًا إِلَّا بَلَغْتُهُ وَلَا أَرَادَنِي أَحَدٌ إِلَّا نَجَوْتُ عَلَيْهِ فَدُونَكَ فَخُذْهُ.

فَأَعْرَضَ عَنْهُ الْحُسَيْنُ عليه السلام بِوَجْهِهِ ثُمَّ قَالَ لَا حَاجَةَ لَنَا فِيكَ وَلَا فِي فَرَسِكَ وَما كُنْتُ مُتَّخِذَ الْمُضِلِّينَ عَضُداً وَلٰكِنْ فِرَّ فَلَا لَنَا وَلَا عَلَيْنَا فَإِنَّهُ مَنْ سَمِعَ وَاعِيَتَنَا أَهْلَ الْبَيْتِ ثُمَّ لَمْ يُجِبْنَا كَبَّهُ اللّٰهُ عَلَى وَجْهِهِ فِي نَارِ جَهَنَّمَ.

ثُمَّ سَارَ حَتَّى نَزَلَ كَرْبَلَاءَ فَقَالَ أَيُّ مَوْضِعٍ هٰذَا.

فَقِيلَ هٰذَا كَرْبَلَاءُ يَا ابْنَ رَسُولِ اللّٰهِ.

فَقَالَ هٰذَا وَاللّٰهِ يَوْمُ كَرْبٍ وَبَلَاءٍ وَهٰذَا الْمَوْضِعُ الَّذِي يُهَرَاقُ فِيهِ دِمَاؤُنَا وَيُبَاحُ فِيهِ حَرِيمُنَا.

فَأَقْبَلَ عُبَيْدُ اللّٰهِ بْنُ زِيَادٍ بِعَسْكَرِهِ حَتَّى عَسْكَرَ بِالنُّخَيْلَةِ وَبَعَثَ إِلَى الْحُسَيْنِ عليه السلام رَجُلًا يُقَالُ لَهُ عُمَرُ بْنُ سَعْدٍ فِي أَرْبَعَةِ آلَافِ فَارِسٍ.

وَأَقْبَلَ عَبْدُ اللهِ بْنُ الْحُصَيْنِ التَّمِيمِيُّ فِي أَلْفِ فَارِسٍ يَتْبَعُهُ شَبَثُ بْنُ رِبْعِيٍّ فِي أَلْفِ فَارِسٍ وَمُحَمَّدُ بْنُ الْأَشْعَثِ بْنِ قَيْسٍ الْكِنْدِيُّ أَيْضًا فِي أَلْفِ فَارِسٍ وَكَتَبَ لِعُمَرَ بْنِ سَعْدٍ عَلَى النَّاسِ وَأَمَرَهُمْ أَنْ يَسْمَعُوا لَهُ وَيُطِيعُوهُ.

فَبَلَغَ عُبَيْدَ اللهِ بْنَ زِيَادٍ أَنَّ عُمَرَ بْنَ سَعْدٍ يُسَامِرُ الْحُسَيْنَ عليه السلام وَيُحَدِّثُهُ وَيَكْرَهُ قِتَالَهُ فَوَجَّهَ إِلَيْهِ شِمْرَ بْنَ ذِي الْجَوْشَنِ فِي أَرْبَعَةِ آلَافِ فَارِسٍ وَكَتَبَ إِلَى عُمَرَ بْنِ سَعْدٍ إِذَا أَتَاكَ كِتَابِي هٰذَا فَلَا تُمْهِلَنَّ الْحُسَيْنَ بْنَ عَلِيٍّ وَخُذْ بِكَظَمِهِ وَحُلْ بَيْنَ الْمَاءِ وَبَيْنَهُ كَمَا حِيلَ بَيْنَ عُثْمَانَ وَبَيْنَ الْمَاءِ يَوْمَ الدَّارِ.

فَلَمَّا وَصَلَ الْكِتَابُ إِلَى عُمَرَ بْنِ سَعْدٍ لَعَنَهُ اللهُ أَمَرَ مُنَادِيَهُ فَنَادَى إِنَّا قَدْ أَجَّلْنَا حُسَيْنًا وَأَصْحَابَهُ يَوْمَهُمْ وَلَيْلَتَهُمْ.

فَشَقَّ ذٰلِكَ عَلَى الْحُسَيْنِ عليه السلام وَعَلَى أَصْحَابِهِ فَقَامَ الْحُسَيْنُ عليه السلام فِي أَصْحَابِهِ خَطِيبًا فَقَالَ اللّٰهُمَّ إِنِّي لَا أَعْرِفُ أَهْلَ بَيْتٍ أَبَرَّ وَلَا أَزْكَى وَلَا أَطْهَرَ مِنْ أَهْلِ بَيْتِي وَلَا أَصْحَابًا هُمْ خَيْرٌ مِنْ أَصْحَابِي وَقَدْ نَزَلَ بِي مَا قَدْ تَرَوْنَ وَأَنْتُمْ فِي حِلٍّ مِنْ بَيْعَتِي لَيْسَتْ لِي فِي أَعْنَاقِكُمْ بَيْعَةٌ وَلَا لِي

عَلَيْكُمْ ذِمَّةٌ وَهٰذَا اللَّيْلُ قَدْ غَشِيَكُمْ فَاتَّخِذُوهُ جَمَلًا وَتَفَرَّقُوا فِي سَوَادِهِ فَإِنَّ الْقَوْمَ إِنَّمَا يَطْلُبُونِّي وَلَوْ ظَفِرُوا بِي لَذَهَلُوا عَنْ طَلَبِ غَيْرِي.

فَقَامَ إِلَيْهِ عَبْدُ اللهِ بْنُ مُسْلِمِ بْنِ عَقِيلِ بْنِ أَبِي طَالِبٍ فَقَالَ يَا ابْنَ رَسُولِ اللهِ مَا ذَا يَقُولُ لَنَا النَّاسُ إِنْ نَحْنُ خَذَلْنَا شَيْخَنَا وَكَبِيرَنَا وَسَيِّدَنَا وَابْنَ سَيِّدِ الْأَعْمَامِ وَابْنَ نَبِيِّنَا سَيِّدِ الْأَنْبِيَاءِ لَمْ نَضْرِبْ مَعَهُ بِسَيْفٍ وَلَمْ نُقَاتِلْ مَعَهُ بِرُمْحٍ لَا وَاللهِ أَوْ نَرِدَ مَوْرِدَكَ وَنَجْعَلَ أَنْفُسَنَا دُونَ نَفْسِكَ وَدِمَاءَنَا دُونَ دَمِكَ فَإِذَا نَحْنُ فَعَلْنَا ذٰلِكَ فَقَدْ قَضَيْنَا مَا عَلَيْنَا وَخَرَجْنَا مِمَّا لَزِمَنَا.

وَقَامَ إِلَيْهِ رَجُلٌ يُقَالُ لَهُ زُهَيْرُ بْنُ الْقَيْنِ الْبَجَلِيُّ فَقَالَ يَا ابْنَ رَسُولِ اللهِ وَدِدْتُ أَنِّي قُتِلْتُ ثُمَّ نُشِرْتُ ثُمَّ قُتِلْتُ ثُمَّ نُشِرْتُ ثُمَّ قُتِلْتُ ثُمَّ نُشِرْتُ فِيكَ وَفِي الَّذِينَ مَعَكَ مِائَةَ قَتْلَةٍ وَإِنَّ اللهَ دَفَعَ بِي عَنْكُمْ أَهْلَ الْبَيْتِ.

فَقَالَ لَهُ وَلِأَصْحَابِهِ جُزِيتُمْ خَيْراً.

ثُمَّ إِنَّ الْحُسَيْنَ عليه السلام أَمَرَ بِحَفِيرَةٍ فَحُفِرَتْ حَوْلَ عَسْكَرِهِ شِبْهَ الْخَنْدَقِ وَأَمَرَ فَحُشِيَتْ حَطَبًا.

وَأَرْسَلَ عَلِيًّا ابْنَهُ عليه السلام فِي ثَلَاثِينَ فَارِسًا وَعِشْرِينَ رَاجِلًا لِيَسْتَقُوا الْمَاءَ

وَهُمْ عَلَى وَجَلٍ شَدِيدٍ وَأَنْشَأَ الْحُسَيْنُ عليه السلام يَقُولُ:

يَا دَهْرُ أُفٍّ لَكَ مِنْ خَلِيلِ كَمْ لَكَ فِي الْإِشْرَاقِ وَالْأَصِيلِ

مِنْ طَالِبٍ وَصَاحِبٍ قَتِيلِ وَالدَّهْرُ لَا يَقْنَعُ بِالْبَدِيلِ

وَإِنَّمَا الْأَمْرُ إِلَى الْجَلِيلِ وَكُلُّ حَيٍّ سَالِكٌ سَبِيلِي

ثُمَّ قَالَ لِأَصْحَابِهِ قُومُوا فَاشْرَبُوا مِنَ الْمَاءِ يَكُنْ آخِرَ زَادِكُمْ وَتَوَضَّئُوا وَاغْتَسِلُوا وَاغْسِلُوا ثِيَابَكُمْ لِتَكُونَ أَكْفَانَكُمْ.

ثُمَّ صَلَّى بِهِمُ الْفَجْرَ وَعَبَّأَهُمْ تَعْبِئَةَ الْحَرْبِ وَأَمَرَ بِحَفِيرَتِهِ الَّتِي حَوْلَ عَسْكَرِهِ فَأُضْرِمَتْ بِالنَّارِ لِيُقَاتِلَ الْقَوْمَ مِنْ وَجْهٍ وَاحِدٍ.

وَأَقْبَلَ رَجُلٌ مِنْ عَسْكَرِ عُمَرَ بْنِ سَعْدٍ عَلَى فَرَسٍ لَهُ يُقَالُ لَهُ ابْنُ أَبِي جُوَيْرِيَةَ الْمُزَنِيُّ فَلَمَّا نَظَرَ إِلَى النَّارِ تَتَّقِدُ صَفَقَ بِيَدِهِ وَنَادَى يَا حُسَيْنُ وَأَصْحَابَ الْحُسَيْنِ أَبْشِرُوا بِالنَّارِ فَقَدْ تَعَجَّلْتُمُوهَا فِي الدُّنْيَا.

فَقَالَ الْحُسَيْنُ عليه السلام مَنِ الرَّجُلُ.

فَقِيلَ ابْنُ أَبِي جُوَيْرِيَةَ الْمُزَنِيُّ فَقَالَ الْحُسَيْنُ عليه‌السلام اَللَّهُمَّ أَذِقْهُ عَذَابَ النَّارِ فِي الدُّنْيَا.

فَنَفَرَ بِهِ فَرَسُهُ فَأَلْقَاهُ فِي تِلْكَ النَّارِ فَاحْتَرَقَ.

ثُمَّ بَرَزَ مِنْ عَسْكَرِ عُمَرَ بْنِ سَعْدٍ رَجُلٌ آخَرُ يُقَالُ لَهُ تَمِيمُ بْنُ الْحُصَيْنِ الْفَزَارِيُّ فَنَادَى يَا حُسَيْنُ وَيَا أَصْحَابَ الْحُسَيْنِ أَ مَا تَرَوْنَ إِلَى مَاءِ الْفُرَاتِ يَلُوحُ كَأَنَّهُ بُطُونُ الْحَيَّاتِ [الْحِيتَانِ] وَاللهِ لَا ذُقْتُمْ مِنْهُ قَطْرَةً حَتَّى تَذُوقُوا الْمَوْتَ جَزَعًا.

فَقَالَ الْحُسَيْنُ عليه‌السلام مَنِ الرَّجُلُ فَقِيلَ تَمِيمُ بْنُ حُصَيْنٍ.

فَقَالَ الْحُسَيْنُ عليه‌السلام هٰذَا وَأَبُوهُ مِنْ أَهْلِ النَّارِ اللَّهُمَّ اقْتُلْ هٰذَا عَطَشًا فِي هٰذَا الْيَوْمِ.

قَالَ فَخَنَقَهُ الْعَطَشُ حَتَّى سَقَطَ عَنْ فَرَسِهِ فَوَطِئَتْهُ الْخَيْلُ بِسَنَابِكِهَا فَمَاتَ.

ثُمَّ أَقْبَلَ آخَرُ مِنْ عَسْكَرِ عُمَرَ بْنِ سَعْدٍ يُقَالُ لَهُ مُحَمَّدُ بْنُ أَشْعَثَ بْنِ قَيْسٍ الْكِنْدِيُّ فَقَالَ يَا حُسَيْنَ بْنَ فَاطِمَةَ أَيَّةُ حُرْمَةٍ لَكَ مِنْ رَسُولِ اللهِ لَيْسَتْ لِغَيْرِكَ.

قَالَ الْحُسَيْنُ عليه السلام هٰذِهِ الآيَةُ إِنَّ اللّٰهَ اصْطَفَى آدَمَ وَنُوحًا وَآلَ إِبْراهِيمَ وَآلَ عِمْرانَ عَلَى الْعَالَمِينَ ذُرِّيَّةً الآيَةَ. ثُمَّ قَالَ وَاللّٰهِ إِنَّ مُحَمَّدًا لَمِنْ آلِ إِبْرَاهِيمَ وَإِنَّ الْعِتْرَةَ الْهَادِيَةَ لَمِنْ آلِ مُحَمَّدٍ مَنِ الرَّجُلُ.

فَقِيلَ مُحَمَّدُ بْنُ أَشْعَثَ بْنِ قَيْسٍ الْكِنْدِيُّ.

فَرَفَعَ الْحُسَيْنُ عليه السلام رَأْسَهُ إِلَى السَّمَاءِ فَقَالَ اللّٰهُمَّ أَرِ مُحَمَّدَ بْنَ الْأَشْعَثِ ذُلًّا فِي هٰذَا الْيَوْمِ لَا تُعِزُّهُ بَعْدَ هٰذَا الْيَوْمِ أَبَدًا.

فَعَرَضَ لَهُ عَارِضٌ فَخَرَجَ مِنَ الْعَسْكَرِ يَتَبَرَّزُ فَسَلَّطَ اللّٰهُ عَلَيْهِ عَقْرَبًا فَلَدَغَهُ فَمَاتَ بَادِيَ الْعَوْرَةِ.

فَبَلَغَ الْعَطَشُ مِنَ الْحُسَيْنِ عليه السلام وَأَصْحَابِهِ فَدَخَلَ عَلَيْهِ رَجُلٌ مِنْ شِيعَتِهِ يُقَالُ لَهُ يَزِيدُ بْنُ الْحُصَيْنِ الْهَمْدَانِيُّ قَالَ إِبْرَاهِيمُ بْنُ عَبْدِ اللّٰهِ رَاوِي الْحَدِيثِ هُوَخَالُ أَبِي إِسْحَاقَ الْهَمْدَانِيِّ.

فَقَالَ يَا ابْنَ رَسُولِ اللّٰهِ أَ تَأْذَنُ لِي فَأَخْرُجَ إِلَيْهِمْ فَأُكَلِّمَهُمْ.

فَأَذِنَ لَهُ فَخَرَجَ إِلَيْهِمْ فَقَالَ يَا مَعْشَرَ النَّاسِ إِنَّ اللّٰهَ عَزَّ وَجَلَّ بَعَثَ مُحَمَّدًا بِالْحَقِّ بَشِيرًا وَنَذِيرًا وَداعِيًا إِلَى اللّٰهِ بِإِذْنِهِ وَسِراجًا مُنِيرًا وَهٰذَا مَاءُ الْفُرَاتِ تَقَعُ فِيهِ خَنَازِيرُ السَّوَادِ وَكِلَابُهَا وَقَدْ حِيلَ بَيْنَهُ وَبَيْنَ ابْنِهِ.

فَقَالُوا يَا يَزِيدُ فَقَدْ أَكْثَرْتَ الْكَلَامَ فَاكْفُفْ فَوَاللّٰهِ لَيَعْطِشُ الْحُسَيْنُ كَمَا عَطَشَ مَنْ كَانَ قَبْلَهُ.

فَقَالَ الْحُسَيْنُ اقْعُدْ يَا يَزِيدُ ثُمَّ وَثَبَ الْحُسَيْنُ ﵇ مُتَوَكِّئًا عَلَى سَيْفِهِ فَنَادَى بِأَعْلَى صَوْتِهِ فَقَالَ أَنْشُدُكُمُ اللّٰهَ هَلْ تَعْرِفُونِّي.

قَالُوا نَعَمْ أَنْتَ ابْنُ رَسُولِ اللّٰهِ وَسِبْطُهُ.

قَالَ أَنْشُدُكُمُ اللّٰهَ هَلْ تَعْلَمُونَ أَنَّ جَدِّي رَسُولُ اللّٰهِ ﷺ.

قَالُوا اللّٰهُمَّ نَعَمْ.

قَالَ أَنْشُدُكُمُ اللّٰهَ هَلْ تَعْلَمُونَ أَنَّ أُمِّي فَاطِمَةُ بِنْتُ مُحَمَّدٍ.

قَالُوا اللّٰهُمَّ نَعَمْ.

قَالَ أَنْشُدُكُمُ اللّٰهَ هَلْ تَعْلَمُونَ أَنَّ أَبِي عَلِيُّ بْنُ أَبِي طَالِبٍ.

قَالُوا اللّٰهُمَّ نَعَمْ.

قَالَ أَنْشُدُكُمُ اللّٰهَ هَلْ تَعْلَمُونَ أَنَّ جَدَّتِي خَدِيجَةُ بِنْتُ خُوَيْلِدٍ أَوَّلُ نِسَاءِ هٰذِهِ الْأُمَّةِ إِسْلَامًا.

قَالُوا اللّٰهُمَّ نَعَمْ.

قَالَ أَنْشُدُكُمُ اللّٰهَ هَلْ تَعْلَمُونَ أَنَّ سَيِّدَ الشُّهَدَاءِ حَمْزَةَ عَمُّ أَبِي.

قَالُوا اللّٰهُمَّ نَعَمْ.

قَالَ فَأَنْشُدُكُمُ اللّٰهَ هَلْ تَعْلَمُونَ أَنَّ جَعْفَرَ الطَّيَّارِ فِي الْجَنَّةِ عَمِّي.

قَالُوا اللّٰهُمَّ نَعَمْ.

قَالَ فَأَنْشُدُكُمُ اللّٰهَ هَلْ تَعْلَمُونَ أَنَّ هٰذَا سَيْفُ رَسُولِ اللّٰهِ وَأَنَا مُتَقَلِّدُهُ.

قَالُوا اللّٰهُمَّ نَعَمْ.

قَالَ فَأَنْشُدُكُمُ اللّٰهَ هَلْ تَعْلَمُونَ أَنَّ هٰذِهِ عِمَامَةُ رَسُولِ اللّٰهِ أَنَا لَابِسُهَا.

قَالُوا اللّٰهُمَّ نَعَمْ.

قَالَ فَأَنْشُدُكُمُ اللّٰهَ هَلْ تَعْلَمُونَ أَنَّ عَلِيًّا كَانَ أَوَّلَهُمْ إِسْلَامًا وَأَعْلَمَهُمْ عِلْمًا وَأَعْظَمَهُمْ حِلْمًا وَأَنَّهُ وَلِيُّ كُلِّ مُؤْمِنٍ وَمُؤْمِنَةٍ.

قَالُوا اللّٰهُمَّ نَعَمْ.

قَالَ فَبِمَ تَسْتَحِلُّونَ دَمِي وَأَبِي الذَّائِدُ عَنِ الْحَوْضِ غَدًا يَذُودُ عَنْهُ رِجَالًا كَمَا يُذَادُ الْبَعِيرُ الصَّادِرُ عَنِ الْمَاءِ وَلِوَاءُ الْحَمْدِ فِي يَدِ جَدِّي يَوْمَ الْقِيَامَةِ.

قَالُوا قَدْ عَلِمْنَا ذٰلِكَ كُلَّهُ وَنَحْنُ غَيْرُ تَارِكِيكَ حَتَّى تَذُوقَ الْمَوْتَ عَطَشًا.

فَأَخَذَ الْحُسَيْنُ ﷷ بِطَرَفِ لِحْيَتِهِ وَهُوَ يَوْمَئِذٍ ابْنُ سَبْعٍ وَخَمْسِينَ سَنَةً. ثُمَّ قَالَ اشْتَدَّ غَضَبُ اللهِ عَلَى الْيَهُودِ حِينَ قَالُوا عُزَيْرٌ ابْنُ اللهِ وَاشْتَدَّ غَضَبُ اللهِ عَلَى النَّصَارَى حِينَ قَالُوا الْمَسِيحُ ابْنُ اللهِ وَاشْتَدَّ غَضَبُ اللهِ عَلَى الْمَجُوسِ حِينَ عَبَدُوا النَّارَ مِنْ دُونِ اللهِ وَاشْتَدَّ غَضَبُ اللهِ عَلَى قَوْمٍ قَتَلُوا نَبِيَّهُمْ وَاشْتَدَّ غَضَبُ اللهِ عَلَى هٰذِهِ الْعِصَابَةِ الَّذِينَ يُرِيدُونَ قَتْلَ ابْنِ نَبِيِّهِمْ.

قَالَ فَضَرَبَ الْحُرُّ بْنُ يَزِيدَ فَرَسَهُ وَجَازَ عَسْكَرَ عُمَرَ بْنِ سَعْدٍ لَعَنَهُ اللهُ إِلَى عَسْكَرِ الْحُسَيْنِ ﷷ وَاضِعًا يَدَهُ عَلَى رَأْسِهِ وَهُوَ يَقُولُ اللّٰهُمَّ إِلَيْكَ أُنِيبُ [أَنَبْتُ] فَتُبْ عَلَيَّ فَقَدْ أَرْعَبْتُ قُلُوبَ أَوْلِيَائِكَ وَأَوْلَادَ نَبِيِّكَ يَا ابْنَ رَسُولِ اللهِ هَلْ لِي مِنْ تَوْبَةٍ.

قَالَ نَعَمْ تَابَ اللهُ عَلَيْكَ.

قَالَ يَا ابْنَ رَسُولِ اللهِ أَ تَأْذَنُ لِي فَأُقَاتِلَ عَنْكَ فَأَذِنَ لَهُ فَبَرَزَ وَهُوَ يَقُولُ:

أَضْرِبُ فِي أَعْنَاقِكُمْ بِالسَّيْفِ   عَنْ خَيْرِ مَنْ حَلَّ بِلَادَ الْخَيْفِ

فَقَتَلَ مِنْهُمْ ثَمَانِيَةَ عَشَرَ رَجُلًا ثُمَّ قُتِلَ فَأَتَاهُ الْحُسَيْنُ ﷷ وَدَمُهُ يَشْخَبُ.

فَقَالَ بَخٍ بَخٍ يَا حُرُّ أَنْتَ حُرٌّ كَمَا سُمِّيتَ فِي الدُّنْيَا وَالْآخِرَةِ ثُمَّ أَنْشَأَ الْحُسَيْنُ يَقُولُ:

لَنِعْمَ الْحُرُّ حُرُّ بَنِي رِيَاحِ وَنِعْمَ الْحُرُّ عِنْدَ مُخْتَلَفِ الرِّمَاحِ
وَنِعْمَ الْحُرُّ إِذْ نَادَى حُسَيْناً فَجَادَ بِنَفْسِهِ عِنْدَ الصَّبَاحِ

ثُمَّ بَرَزَ مِنْ بَعْدِهِ زُهَيْرُ بْنُ الْقَيْنِ الْبَجَلِيُّ وَهُوَ يَقُولُ مُخَاطِبًا لِلْحُسَيْنِ عليه السلام:

الْيَوْمَ نَلْقَى جَدَّكَ النَّبِيَّا وَحَسَناً وَالْمُرْتَضَى عَلِيّاً

فَقَتَلَ مِنْهُمْ تِسْعَةَ عَشَرَ رَجُلًا ثُمَّ صُرِعَ وَهُوَيَقُولُ:

أَنَا زُهَيْرٌ وَأَنَا ابْنُ الْقَيْنِ أَذُبُّكُمْ بِالسَّيْفِ عَنْ حُسَيْنِ

ثُمَّ بَرَزَ مِنْ بَعْدِهِ حَبِيبُ بْنُ مُظَاهِرٍ [مُظَهِّرٍ] الْأَسَدِيُّ رِضْوَانُ اللهِ عَلَيْهِ وَهُوَ يَقُولُ:

أَنَا حَبِيبٌ وَأَبِي مُظَاهِرٌ لَنَحْنُ أَزْكَى مِنْكُمُ وَأَطْهَرُ
نَنْصُرُ خَيْرَ النَّاسِ حِينَ يُذْكَرُ

فَقَتَلَ مِنْهُمْ أَحَداً وَثَلَاثِينَ رَجُلًا ثُمَّ قُتِلَ رِضْوَانُ اللهِ عَلَيْهِ.

ثُمَّ بَرَزَ مِنْ بَعْدِهِ عَبْدُ اللّٰهِ بْنُ أَبِي عُرْوَةَ الْغِفَارِيُّ وَهُوَ يَقُولُ:

قَدْ عَلِمَتْ حَقًّا بَنُو غِفَارِ أَنِّي أَذُبُّ فِي طِلَابِ الثَّارِ

بِالْمَشْرَفِيِّ وَالْقَنَا الْخَطَّارِ

فَقَتَلَ مِنْهُمْ عِشْرِينَ رَجُلًا ثُمَّ قُتِلَ رَحِمَهُ اللّٰهُ.

ثُمَّ بَرَزَ مِنْ بَعْدِهِ بُرَيْرُ [بُدَيْرُ] بْنُ خُضَيْرٍ الْهَمْدَانِيُّ وَكَانَ أَقْرَأَ أَهْلِ زَمَانِهِ وَهُوَ يَقُولُ:

أَنَا بُرَيْرٌ وَأَبِي خُضَيْرٌ لَا خَيْرَ فِيمَنْ لَيْسَ فِيهِ خَيْرٌ

فَقَتَلَ مِنْهُمْ ثَلَاثِينَ رَجُلًا ثُمَّ قُتِلَ رِضْوَانُ اللّٰهِ عَلَيْهِ ثُمَّ بَرَزَ مِنْ بَعْدِهِ مَالِكُ بْنُ أَنَسٍ الْكَاهِلِيُّ وَهُوَ يَقُولُ:

قَدْ عَلِمَتْ كَاهِلُهَا وَدُودَانُ وَالْخِنْدِفِيُّونَ وَقَيْسُ عَيْلَانَ

بِأَنَّ قَوْمِي قُصَمُ الْأَقْرَانِ يَا قَوْمِ كُونُوا كَأُسُودِ الْجَانِ

آلُ عَلِيٍّ شِيعَةُ الرَّحْمَنِ وَآلُ حَرْبٍ شِيعَةُ الشَّيْطَانِ

فَقَتَلَ مِنْهُمْ ثَمَانِيَةَ عَشَرَ رَجُلًا ثُمَّ قُتِلَ رِضْوَانُ اللّٰهِ عَلَيْهِ.

وَبَرَزَ مِنْ بَعْدِهِ زِيَادُ بْنُ مُهَاصِرٍ [مُهَاجِرٍ] الْكِنْدِيُّ فَحَمَلَ عَلَيْهِمْ وَأَنْشَأَ يَقُولُ:

أَشْجَعُ مِنْ لَيْثِ الْعَرِينِ [الْعَزِيزِ] الْخَادِرِ　　يَا رَبِّ إِنِّي لِلْحُسَيْنِ نَاصِرٌ

وَلِابْنِ سَعْدٍ تَارِكٌ مُهَاجِرٌ

فَقَتَلَ مِنْهُمْ تِسْعَةً ثُمَّ قُتِلَ رِضْوَانُ اللّٰهِ عَلَيْهِ.

وَبَرَزَ مِنْ بَعْدِهِ وَهْبُ بْنُ وَهْبٍ وَكَانَ نَصْرَانِيًّا أَسْلَمَ عَلَى يَدِ الْحُسَيْنِ ﵇ هُوَ وَأُمُّهُ فَاتَّبَعُوهُ إِلَى كَرْبَلَاءَ فَرَكِبَ فَرَسًا وَتَنَاوَلَ بِيَدِهِ عُودَ الْفُسْطَاطِ [عَمُودَ الْفُسْطَاطِ] فَقَاتَلَ وَقَتَلَ مِنَ الْقَوْمِ سَبْعَةً أَوْ ثَمَانِيَةً ثُمَّ اسْتُؤْسِرَ فَأُتِيَ بِهِ عُمَرُ بْنُ سَعْدٍ لَعَنَهُ اللّٰهُ فَأَمَرَ بِضَرْبِ عُنُقِهِ وَرُمِيَ بِهِ إِلَى عَسْكَرِ الْحُسَيْنِ ﵇ وَأَخَذَتْ أُمُّهُ سَيْفَهُ وَبَرَزَتْ فَقَالَ لَهَا الْحُسَيْنُ ﵇ يَا أُمَّ وَهْبٍ اجْلِسِي فَقَدْ وَضَعَ اللّٰهُ الْجِهَادَ عَنِ النِّسَاءِ إِنَّكِ وَابْنَكِ مَعَ جَدِّي مُحَمَّدٍ ﷺ فِي الْجَنَّةِ.

ثُمَّ بَرَزَ مِنْ بَعْدِهِ هِلَالُ بْنُ حَجَّاجٍ وَهُوَ يَقُولُ:

أَرْمِي بِهَا مُعْلَمَةً أَفْوَاقُهَا [أَفْوَاهُهَا]　　وَالنَّفْسُ لَا يَنْفَعُهَا إِشْفَاقُهَا

فَقَتَلَ مِنْهُمْ ثَلَاثَةَ عَشَرَ رَجُلًا ثُمَّ قُتِلَ رِضْوَانُ اللّٰهِ عَلَيْهِ.

وَبَرَزَ مِنْ بَعْدِهِ عَبْدُ اللّٰهِ بْنُ مُسْلِمِ بْنِ عَقِيلِ بْنِ أَبِي طَالِبٍ وَأَنْشَأَ يَقُولُ:

أَقْسَمْتُ لَا أُقْتَلُ إِلَّا حُرًّا وَقَدْ وَجَدْتُ الْمَوْتَ شَيْئًا مُرًّا
أَكْرَهُ أَنْ أُدْعَى جَبَانًا فَرًّا إِنَّ الْجَبَانَ مَنْ عَصَى وَفَرًّا

فَقَتَلَ مِنْهُمْ ثَلَاثَةً ثُمَّ قُتِلَ رِضْوَانُ اللهِ عَلَيْهِ وَرَحْمَتُهُ.

وَبَرَزَ مِنْ بَعْدِهِ عَلِيُّ بْنُ الْحُسَيْنِ عليه السلام فَلَمَّا بَرَزَ إِلَيْهِمْ دَمَعَتْ عَيْنُ الْحُسَيْنِ عليه السلام فَقَالَ اللَّهُمَّ كُنْ أَنْتَ الشَّهِيدَ عَلَيْهِمْ فَقَدْ بَرَزَ إِلَيْهِمُ ابْنُ رَسُولِكَ وَأَشْبَهُ النَّاسِ وَجْهًا وَسَمْتًا بِهِ فَجَعَلَ يَرْتَجِزُ وَهُوَ يَقُولُ:

أَنَا عَلِيُّ بْنُ الْحُسَيْنِ بْنِ عَلِي نَحْنُ وَبَيْتِ اللهِ أَوْلَى بِالنَّبِي
أَ مَا تَرَوْنَ كَيْفَ أَحْمِي عَنْ أَبِي

فَقَتَلَ مِنْهُمْ عَشَرَةً ثُمَّ رَجَعَ إِلَى أَبِيهِ فَقَالَ يَا أَبَتِ الْعَطَشَ فَقَالَ لَهُ الْحُسَيْنُ عليه السلام صَبْرًا يَا بُنَيَّ يَسْقِيكَ جَدُّكَ بِالْكَأْسِ الْأَوْفَى فَرَجَعَ فَقَاتَلَ حَتَّى قَتَلَ مِنْهُمْ أَرْبَعَةً وَأَرْبَعِينَ رَجُلًا ثُمَّ قُتِلَ وَبَرَزَ مِنْ بَعْدِهِ الْقَاسِمُ بْنُ الْحَسَنِ بْنِ عَلِيٍّ عليه السلام وَهُوَ يَقُولُ:

لَا تَجْزَعِي نَفْسِي فَكُلٌّ فَانِ الْيَوْمَ تَلْقَيْنَ ذُرَى الْجِنَانِ

فَقَتَلَ مِنْهُمْ ثَلَاثَةً ثُمَّ رُمِيَ عَنْ فَرَسِهِ رِضْوَانُ اللهِ عَلَيْهِ وَصَلَوَاتُهُ.

وَنظَرَ الْحُسَيْنُ عليه السلام يَمِينًا وَشِمَالًا وَلَا يَرَى أَحَدًا فَرَفَعَ رَأْسَهُ إِلَى السَّمَاءِ فَقَالَ اللّٰهُمَّ إِنَّكَ تَرَى مَا يُصْنَعُ بِوَلَدِ نَبِيِّكَ.

وَحَالَ بَنُو كِلَابٍ بَيْنَهُ وَبَيْنَ الْمَاءِ وَرُمِيَ بِسَهْمٍ فَوَقَعَ فِي نَحْرِهِ وَخَرَّ عَنْ فَرَسِهِ.

فَأَخَذَ السَّهْمَ فَرَمَى بِهِ وَجَعَلَ يَتَلَقَّى الدَّمَ بِكَفِّهِ فَلَمَّا امْتَلَأَتْ لَطَخَ بِهَا رَأْسَهُ وَلِحْيَتَهُ وَيَقُولُ أَلْقَى اللّٰهَ عَزَّ وَجَلَّ وَأَنَا مَظْلُومٌ مُتَلَطِّخٌ بِدَمِي.

ثُمَّ خَرَّ عَلَى خَدِّهِ الْأَيْسَرِ صَرِيعًا وَأَقْبَلَ عَدُوُّ اللّٰهِ سِنَانٌ الْإِيَادِيُّ وَشِمْرُ بْنُ ذِي الْجَوْشَنِ الْعَامِرِيُّ لَعَنَهُ اللّٰهُ فِي رِجَالٍ مِنْ أَهْلِ الشَّامِ حَتَّى وَقَفُوا عَلَى رَأْسِ الْحُسَيْنِ عليه السلام.

فَقَالَ بَعْضُهُمْ لِبَعْضٍ مَا تَنْتَظِرُونَ أَرِيحُوا الرَّجُلَ.

فَنزَلَ سِنَانُ بْنُ أَنَسٍ الْإِيَادِيُّ لَعَنَهُ اللّٰهُ وَأَخَذَ بِلِحْيَةِ الْحُسَيْنِ عليه السلام وَجَعَلَ يَضْرِبُ بِالسَّيْفِ فِي حَلْقِهِ وَهُوَيَقُولُ وَاللّٰهِ إِنِّي لَأَجْتَزُّ رَأْسَكَ وَأَنَا أَعْلَمُ أَنَّكَ ابْنُ رَسُولِ اللّٰهِ صلى الله عليه وآله وَخَيْرُ النَّاسِ أُمًّا وَأَبًا.

وَأَقْبَلَ فَرَسُ الْحُسَيْنِ عليه السلام حَتَّى لَطَخَ عُرْفَهُ وَنَاصِيَتَهُ بِدَمِ الْحُسَيْنِ وَجَعَلَ يَرْكُضُ وَيَصْهَلُ فَسَمِعَتْ بَنَاتُ النَّبِيِّ صلى الله عليه وآله صَهِيلَهُ فَخَرَجْنَ فَإِذَا الْفَرَسُ بِلَا رَاكِبٍ فَعَرَفْنَ أَنَّ حُسَيْنًا عليه السلام قَدْ قُتِلَ.

وَخَرَجَتْ أُمُّ كُلْثُومٍ بِنْتُ الْحُسَيْنِ وَاضِعَةً يَدَهَا عَلَى رَأْسِهَا تَنْدُبُ وَتَقُولُ وَا مُحَمَّدَاهْ هٰذَا الْحُسَيْنُ بِالْعَرَاءِ قَدْ سُلِبَ الْعِمَامَةَ وَالرِّدَاءَ.

وَأَقْبَلَ سِنَانٌ لَعَنَهُ اللّٰهُ حَتَّى أَدْخَلَ رَأْسَ الْحُسَيْنِ بْنِ عَلِيٍّ عليه السلام عَلَى عُبَيْدِ اللّٰهِ بْنِ زِيَادٍ لَعَنَهُ اللّٰهُ وَهُوَ يَقُولُ:

امْلَأْ رِكَابِي فِضَّةً وَذَهَبًا — إِنِّي قَتَلْتُ الْمَلِكَ الْمُحَجَّبَا

قَتَلْتُ خَيْرَ النَّاسِ أُمًّا وَأَبًا — وَخَيْرَهُمْ إِذْ يُنْسَبُونَ نَسَبًا

فَقَالَ لَهُ عُبَيْدُ اللّٰهِ بْنُ زِيَادٍ وَيْحَكَ فَإِنْ عَلِمْتَ أَنَّهُ خَيْرُ النَّاسِ أَبًا وَأُمًّا لِمَ قَتَلْتَهُ إِذًا فَأَمَرَ بِهِ فَضُرِبَ عُنُقُهُ وَعَجَّلَ اللّٰهُ بِرُوحِهِ إِلَى النَّارِ.

وَأَرْسَلَ ابْنُ زِيَادٍ لَعَنَهُ اللّٰهُ قَاصِدًا إِلَى أُمِّ كُلْثُومٍ [أُخْتِ] بِنْتِ الْحُسَيْنِ عليهما السلام فَقَالَ الْحَمْدُ لِلّٰهِ الَّذِي قَتَلَ رِجَالَكُمْ فَكَيْفَ تَرَوْنَ مَا فَعَلَ بِكُمْ.

فَقَالَتْ يَا ابْنَ زِيَادٍ لَئِنْ قَرَّتْ عَيْنُكَ بِقَتْلِ الْحُسَيْنِ ﵇ فَطَالَ مَا قَرَّتْ عَيْنُ جَدِّهِ بِهِ وَكَانَ يُقَبِّلُهُ وَيَلْثِمُ شَفَتَيْهِ وَيَضَعُهُ عَلَى عَاتِقِهِ يَا ابْنَ زِيَادٍ أَعِدَّ لِجَدِّهِ جَوَاباً فَإِنَّهُ خَصْمُكَ غَداً.

Our Other Publications[1]

1. *A Land Most Goodly: The Story of Yemen in the Quran and in the Times of Prophet Muḥammad and Imam ʿAlī ibn Abī Ṭālib* by Jaffer Ladak
2. *A Star Amongst the Stars: The life and times of the great companion: Jabir ibn Abdullah al-Ansari* by Jaffer Ladak
3. *Alif, Baa, Taa of Kerbala* by Saleem Bhimji, and Arifa Hudda
4. *Arbāʿīn of Imam Ḥusayn* compiled and translated by Saleem Bhimji
5. *Contentious Issues in Islamic History - ʿUmar ibn al-Khaṭṭāb* written by Saeed Dawari and translated by Saleem Bhimji
6. *Deficient? A Review of Sermon 80 from Nahj al-Balāgha* by Āyatullāh al-ʿUẓmā Shaykh Nāṣir Makārim Shīrāzī and translated by Saleem Bhimji

---

[1] The following is a list of all original writings and translations from the Islamic Publishing House. As the majority of these titles are out of stock, we are re-releasing all our works via Print-on-Demand through Amazon.

Search for the title that you are looking for via Amazon on one of their international platforms, including: Australia, Canada, France, Germany, Italy, Japan, UK, USA, Netherlands, and Spain.

If you cannot find any of the above titles on Amazon, feel free to email us at *iph@iph.ca*.

7. *Exegesis of the 29th Juz of the Qur'ān - a translation of Tafsīr Namuneh* by Āyatullāh al-'Uẓmā Shaykh Nāṣir Makārim Shīrāzī and translated by Saleem Bhimji
8. *Foundations of Islamic Unity* - a translation of *Al-Fuṣūl Al-Muhimmah fī Ta'līf al-Ummah* by 'Abd al-Ḥusayn Sharaf al-Dīn al-Mūsawī al-'Āmilī and translated by Batool Ispahany
9. *Fountain of Paradise - Fāṭima az-Zahrā' in the Noble Quran* by Āyatullāh al-'Uẓmā Shaykh Nāṣir Makārim Shīrāzī, compiled and translated by Saleem Bhimji
10. *God and god of Science* by Syed Hasan Raza Jafri
11. *House of Sorrows* by Shaykh 'Abbās al-Qummī and translated by Aejaz Ali Turab Husayn Husayni
12. *Inspirational Insights* by Mohammed Khaku
13. *Islam and Religious Pluralism* by Āyatullāh Shaykh Murtaḍā Muṭahharī and translated by Sayyid Sulayman Ali Hasan
14. *Journey to Eternity - A Handbook of Supplications for the Soul* compiled and translated by Saleem Bhimji and Arifa Hudda
15. *Love and Hate for Allah's Sake* by Mujtaba Saburi translated by Saleem Bhimji
16. *Love for the Family* compiled and translated by Yasin T. Al-Jibouri, Saleem Bhimji, and others

17. *Moral Management* by Abbas Rahimi and translated by Saleem Bhimji
18. *Morals of the Masumeen* by Arifa Hudda
19. *Prayers of the Final Prophet - A collection of supplications of Prophet Muḥammad* by 'Allāmah Sayyid Muḥammad Ḥusayn Ṭabā'ṭabā'ī and translated by Tahir Ridha-Jaffer
20. *Ramaḍān Reflections* compiled by A Group of Muslim Scholars and translated by Saleem Bhimji
21. *Ṣalāt al-Āyāt* by Saleem Bhimji
22. *Ṣalāt al-Ghufaylah: Salvation through Patience & Perseverance* written by Saleem Bhimji
23. *Secrets of the Ḥajj* by Āyatullāh al-'Uẓmā Shaykh Ḥusayn Mazāherī and translated by Saleem Bhimji
24. *Sunan an-Nabī* by 'Allāmah Sayyid Muḥammad Ḥusayn Ṭabā'ṭabā'ī and translated by Tahir Ridha-Jaffer
25. *Tears from Heaven's Flowers: An Anthology of English Poetry about the Ahlulbayt* by Abrahim al-Zubeidi
26. *The Firmest Armament: Commentary on Āyatul Kursī (The Verse of the Throne)* by Sayyid Nasrullah Burujerdi and translated by Saleem Bhimji

27. *The Last Luminary and Ways to Delve into the Light* by Sayyid Muhammad Ridha Husayni Mutlaq and translated by Saleem Bhimji
28. *The Muslim Legal Will Booklet* by Saleem Bhimji
29. *The Pure Life* by Āyatullāh al-'Uẓmā as-Sayyid Muḥammad Taqī al-Modarresī and translated by Jaffer Ladak with commentary by Dr. Zainali Panjwani and Jaffer Ladak
30. *The Third Testimony: Imam 'Alī in the Adhān* compiled and translated by Saleem Bhimji
31. *The Torch of Perpetual Guidance - A Brief Commentary on Ziyārat al-'Āshūrā'* by Abbas Azizi and translated by Saleem Bhimji
32. *Weapon of the Believer* by 'Allāmah Muḥammad Bāqir Majlisī and translated by Saleem Bhimji

In addition to these titles which are currently available, look for our series of booklets featuring the commentary of the Noble Quran entitled *Living the Quran Through The Living Quran – A Translation of Tafsīr Nūr* of Shaykh Muḥsin Qarā'atī. This series of booklets will be available exclusively from Amazon.

www.ingramcontent.com/pod-product-compliance
Lightning Source LLC
Chambersburg PA
CBHW021913040426
42447CB00007B/833
* 9 7 8 1 9 2 7 9 3 0 4 2 7 *